Gaston Eyskens
Lecture Series

Dollars, Debts, and Deficits, Rudiger Dornbusch, 1986

Geography and Trade, Paul Krugman, 1991

Marshall's Tendencies: What Can Economists Know? John
Sutton, 2000

Marshall's Tendencies

Marshall's Tendencies

What Can Economists
Know?

John Sutton

Published jointly by
Leuven University Press
Leuven, Belgium
and
The MIT Press
Cambridge, Massachusetts
London, England

© 2000 Massachusetts Institute of Technology

This book was set in Palatino on '3B2' by Asco Typesetters, Hong Kong. Printed and bound in the United States of America.

Ordering Information: All orders from Belgium, the Netherlands, and Luxembourg should be sent to Leuven University Press (ISBN: 90 5867 047 3; D/2000/1869/44).

Library of Congress Cataloging-in-Publication Data

Sutton, John, 1948–
  Marshall's tendencies : what can economists know? / John Sutton.
     p.   cm. — (Gaston Eyskens lecture series)
  Includes bibliographical references and index.
  ISBN 0-262-19442-2 (hc.)
  1. Economics—Mathematical models. 2. Marshall, Alfred, 1842–1924.
I. Title. II. Series.
HB135.S825   2000
330—dc21   00-029196

To Jean

A human loves an explanation, and if a good one is not available, a bad one will be confabulated. We see patterns where there are none, and plan our actions around them.

—Roger Scruton

Contents

Series Foreword

The "Professor Dr. Gaston Eyskens Lectures" are published under the auspices of the chair established on the occasion of the promotion of Professor Doctor Gaston Eyskens to Professor Emeritus on 4 October 1975 and named after him. This chair is intended to promote the teaching of theoretical and applied economics by organizing biannually a series of lectures to be given by outstanding scholars.

The pursuance of this goal is made possible through an endowment fund established by numerous Belgian institutions and associations as an expression of their great appreciation for the long and fruitful teaching career of Professor Gaston Eyskens.

Born on 1 April 1905, Gaston Eyskens has taught at the Catholic University of Leuven since 1931. For an unusually large number of student generations Professor Eyskens has been the inspiring teacher of general economics, public finance, and macroeconomic theory. He is recognized as the founder of Dutch language economic education in Leuven. It should also be mentioned that he was a founder of the Center for Economic Studies of the Department of Economics. As a member of the governing board of the university from 1954 to 1968, he succeeded in adding an important dimension to the social service task of the university.

As member of parliament, minister, and head of government, he dominated the Belgian political scene for many years. His influence on the cultural and economic emancipation of the Flemish community has been enormous.

Professor Dr. P. Van Cayseele

Chairman of the Administrative Committee of the Gaston Eyskens Chair

Acknowledgments

In 1931, Lionel Robbins wrote a little book entitled *An Essay on the Nature and Significance of Economic Science*, in which he argued the case for the value of theory in economics. I was reminded of Robbins's book when, in 1995, I was asked on the occasion of the London School of Economics' centenary to give a talk on economics to some of the school's alumni. The invitation to give the Eyskens Lectures for 1996 offered me an opportunity to develop the theme of that lecture at greater length. My thanks are due to my hosts in the Industrial Organization group at the University of Leuven for their many helpful suggestions.

For their comments on the first draft of these lectures, I would like to thank Charlie Bean, Adam Brandenburger, Tore Ellingsen, Richard Freeman, Lennart Hjalmarsson, Steve Klepper, Tim Leunig, Steve Nickell, Volker Nocke, Neil Pratt, Mark Schankerman, Silvia Sonderegger, Jian Tong, Lucia Tsai, Tommaso Valletti, and Leopoldo Yanes.

Preface

The student who comes to economics for the first time is apt to raise two rather obvious questions. The first relates to the economist's habit of assuming that individuals and firms can be treated as "rational maximizers," whose behavior amounts to choosing the action that maximizes some simple objective function such as utility or profit. Are people that simple? The second beginner's question relates to the economist's habit of reducing the discussion of some messy and complex issue to a simple mathematical model that purports to capture the essential features of the situation. To what extent is such a simple representation helpful rather than misleading?

By the time that students have advanced a couple of years into their studies, both these questions are forgotten. Those students who remain troubled by them have quit the field; those who remain are socialized and no longer ask about such things. Yet these are deep questions, which cut to the very heart of the subject.

It is the second of these beginner's questions I explore in these lectures. I want to ask: is it possible to find economic models that work? Regarding the other question, much has been said in the recent research literature, and I will have little to say on this issue here. Nonetheless, these two beginner's questions are deeply intertwined, and in addressing the second, we will cast new light on the first.

In preparing these lectures, I have had in mind an ideal reader: this is someone who already knows, from studying other fields, how a successful theory based on formal mathematical models works. But he or she has only recently stumbled upon economics, and though accepting the practical importance of its agenda, is more than a little skeptical as to what may be gained by writing down formal mathematical models in this area ...

1 The Standard Paradigm

The laws of economics are to be compared with the laws of the tides, rather than with the simple and exact law of gravitation. For the actions of men are so various and uncertain, that the best statement of tendencies, which we can make in a science of human conduct, must needs be inexact and faulty.

—Alfred Marshall, *Principles of Economics*

In January 1986, I spent a sabbatical at the University of California at San Diego. On arriving at the airport, I went to look for a taxi. It wasn't hard to find one. Beyond the dozen that sat in line outside the terminal, I could see a whole parking lot full of taxis queuing to join the line. As we drove to La Jolla, the taxi driver told me that there was actually a second lot in which taxis queued to enter the one I had seen. He counted on getting only four fares a day, with a two- to three-hour wait each time. It wasn't hard to see what had gone wrong. The city fathers, responding to the prevailing fashion for "deregulation," had abolished restrictions on the number of licences. Fare levels remained much the same as before, and because entry was unrestricted, new drivers entered the business until the number of fares earned per day drove their incomes down to the same level that the last recruit could have earned in some alternative occupation. The drivers were no better off; San Diegans paid no less for their taxi rides, and lots of empty cabs sat in line for most of the day.

I tell this story not because it is novel, but because it is commonplace. It is typical of a kind of story economists continually stumble upon, and remember. We economists like such examples; by illustrating the unintended consequences of well-meaning policies, they point to the need to understand correctly how certain basic economic mechanisms work—a point I take up in chapter 4, where I return to the story of San Diego's taxicabs.

The economics of San Diego taxicabs can be analyzed quite satisfactorily by looking to some simple qualitative features of the market; there is little need to begin estimating supply and demand schedules. Unfortunately, most of the questions put to economists are less tractable. Suppose, for example, we ask: how will a rise in interest rates affect the level of investment in the economy? We may have a strong theoretical reason to believe that investment will fall. Yet to demonstrate this, or to measure the size of the impact, may prove extremely difficult. Changes in the level of investment will be driven primarily by fluctuations in demand; the expectations of firms—which are notoriously hard to measure directly—will play a key role in driving outcomes; and the impact of changes in interest rates can only be measured by "controlling for" the separate influences exerted by these and other relevant factors. So how do we proceed?

In the first half of the twentieth century, economists began for the first time to bring together formal theoretical models with substantial bodies of empirical data. In so doing, they were faced with the problem of thinking about the gap between their simple theoretical models and the complex and messy world they were attempting to model. In the models, agents were rational maximizers: consumers maximized "utility," firms maximized profit. Markets were described in simple terms: each firm might be represented as a profit-maximizing agent equipped with some production function that defined its output level as a function of inputs supplied, and the firm's task was simply to decide how much of each input to purchase, and how much output to produce. The workings of the market were represented by allowing firms' actions to mesh together in a simple way to generate "equilibrium prices"; and so on. In contrast to this simple model, the world bristled with complexities, many of which ran far beyond the scope of any usefully simple model. How, then, should the predictions of the simple theoretical model be related to the empirical observations thrown up by the world?

By the late 1940s, a paradigm had emerged that offered a coherent basis for jumping between the model and the data. This paradigm has formed the backbone of applied

economics for the past fifty years. It has deep roots, for
its origins can be traced to the book that dominated the
teaching of economics in the first three decades of the century: Alfred Marshall's *Principles of Economics*.

Marshall's Tendencies

Marshall devoted chapter 3 of the *Principles* to a discussion of the nature of "economic laws." Why, he asked,
should the "laws of economics" be less predictable and
precise in their workings than the laws of physics? The
key to Marshall's view lies in his claim that economic
mechanisms work out their influences against a messy
background of complicated factors, so that the most we
can expect of economic analysis is that it captures the
"tendencies" induced by changes in this or that factor. A
rise in demand implies a "tendency" for price to rise in
the sense that, so long as none of the complicating factors
work in the opposite direction with sufficient strength to
cancel its effect, we will see a rise in price. To help the
reader see what is involved in this idea, Marshall introduced in his third edition a homely analogy. The analogy
seemed apt, and it has cast a long shadow.

The laws of gravity, Marshall noted, work in a highly reg-
ular way: the orbit of Jupiter can be predicted with great
precision. In contrast to this, the movement of the tides is
much harder to predict. The tides are affected by two different influences. The primary influence lies in the gravita-

tional pull of the moon and the sun, and this contribution can be modeled with great accuracy. But the tides are also affected by meteorological factors, and these are notoriously difficult to predict. Fortunately, they are a secondary influence, and by modeling the astronomical factors, we can still arrive at a theory that affords us an adequate prediction, though always one that is subject to some error.

Marshall's analogy lies at the heart of these lectures. It is much richer than might appear at first to be the case. For if the analogy of the tides were valid in economics, life would be much easier for economists. What I am going to suggest is that the analogy of the tides is misleading, in an interesting way. It is not a very good analogy for the economic reality we are trying to model, except under special circumstances, but it offers a nice illustration of a situation in which the standard paradigm of applied economics works perfectly. If Marshall's analogy were valid, we would have seen spectacular progress in economics over the past fifty years (box 1.1).

Marshall's First Critic

For Marshall's contemporaries, the claim that the workings of the market mechanism might pin down a unique outcome as a function of a small number of observable market characteristics, subject to a small "noise" component in the manner suggested by his tides analogy, was a rather bold claim. To those skeptical of theory, it had no merit; but even among the leading advocates of the newly

Box 1.1
Modeling the Tides

When Marshall was writing the *Principles*, the theory of the tides was still in a rather unsatisfactory state. Though it was known from the time of Galileo and Newton that the tides were caused by the gravitational pull of the moon and sun, it was not until Pierre-Simon Laplace solved the basic equations of the system, and showed how the influence of sun and moon could be decomposed into three contributions ("harmonic components"), that the theory assumed its modern form. The work of Sir George Darwin brought the theory to the form that was standard when Marshall wrote the *Principles*.[1]

It was only in the first half of this century that researchers came to appreciate the importance of modeling the tides in each ocean as (approximately independent) standing waves between continents, and the solutions of the associated systems of equations with various simplified representations of the continental "boundaries" led to a new degree of precision in modeling the "astronomical" component.[2] More recently, the main advances in the area came with the accurate modeling of the correction terms that are required to allow for the fact that the ocean is not of a uniform depth ("shallow water effects"); see Pugh 1989.

Though this development of a satisfactory theory of the astronomical component took two centuries, the constant

1. The second son of Charles Darwin. His monumental work, *The Tides and Kindred Phenomena in the Solar System*, appeared in 1898. For an introduction to the theory of the tides as it stood in Marshall's day, see for example Wheeler 1906.
2. For an early account, see for example Johnstone 1923. For a modern review of the theory, see Melchior 1983.

Box 1.1 (continued)

checks provided by observed values under "normal" meteorological conditions provided an excellent empirical testbed for driving steady advances in theory. Today, while modeling the tides is still a major field of research supporting a major journal and a steady flow of monographs, the problem of modeling the height and time of high tide (the "elevation" problem) is essentially solved. The focus of research in the field has now shifted to more subtle problems, such as modeling the way in which the velocity of the flow varies with depth.

developing research program in theory, there were profound differences of view. These differences turned on the question: if we begin with only those few assumptions that we can readily justify, will this provide a model within which a unique outcome is pinned down?

The key exchange was that between Marshall and Francis Edgeworth, and was conducted by reference to the simple context of a single-product market in which a number of rival firms competed. Marshall proceeded conventionally by constructing a supply schedule and computing the intersection of supply and demand as the outcome. Edgeworth chose to proceed more slowly: by asking about the different strategies available to the agents on either side of the market, he arrived at a more pessimistic conclusion. Prices, he claimed, would be indeterminate within a certain region—and only where the numbers of agents in the market became very large, would this region shrink to the unique competitive outcome defined by Marshall. Within the region of indeterminacy, we could not hope to pin down a unique outcome by reference to the observable characteristics of supply and demand.

Now there are two ways of looking at Edgeworth's objection. The first says that there are factors that will determine where we will end up within the zone of indeterminacy, but we don't know much about these factors. Different detailed models may be equally plausible a priori, which would lead us to different outcomes (the "class of models" view). Another way of putting things is to imagine that there exists some supermodel that embodies all the particular models; this supermodel is "more complete" than Edgeworth's in that it contains additional explanatory variables—which index the different constituent models that it encompasses—but these additional variables are not ones we can measure, proxy, or control for in practice (the "unobservability" view). These two versions of Edgeworth's objection are equivalent, and we will see where they lead to in chapter 3.

In the interchange that followed, Marshall's huge prestige carried the day[1]: the best way forward, he felt, was to set aside the difficulties that Edgeworth emphasized as secondary complications. Just proceed by assuming that the world is approximated by a well-behaved model with a

---

1. For a full review of this interchange, see Sutton 1993.

unique equilibrium, and the analogy of the tides holds good; the outcomes we observe are no more than the "true equilibrium" outcome plus some "random noise."

Early Progress

During the 1920s and 1930s, economists began to make substantial strides in bringing together economic theory with empirical data. The approach taken over this period reflected the widespread view that economic datasets could not be validly described by reference to a formal probabilistic model. Rather, the idea was to use a deterministic theoretical model, whose role was to represent the "true" underlying mechanisms; the passage from theoretical predictions to the data was bridged by attributing differences between predicted and actual values to factors omitted from the model, or to errors of measurement. Even though statistical techniques such as the least squares method were sometimes used to estimate an underlying relationship, this procedure was not interpreted by reference to a probabilistic model, so concepts such as the "standard error" of an estimated coefficient were not introduced (Morgan 1987).

Though substantial efforts were devoted to such studies, their role remained controversial. At stake was the issue of whether the relationships uncovered by such exercises had some kind of status that transcended the particular data set under examination. After all, if the factors that lay outside the model were to shift between one dataset and another, then the estimated relationship would shift. Lionel Robbins, in a well-known passage in *An Essay on the Nature and Significance of Economic Science* (1932), satirized the work of a hypothetical "Dr. Blank," who sets out to estimate the demand schedule for herrings. Gathering data on prices and quantities for successive days, it may be possible by "judicious 'doctoring' for seasonal movements, population change, and so on" to estimate the average elasticity of demand over some period. But, Robbins remarks, "there is no reason to suppose that changes in the future will be due to the causes that have operated in the past ... there is no justification for claiming for [these] results the status of the so-called 'statistical' laws of the natural sciences."[2]

Robbins's skepticism went hand in hand with his strongly expressed view as to how far we can proceed on the basis of a priori theoretical arguments. In Robbins's view, the assumptions made by economists at that period were usu-

---

2. Robbins's example of the fish market is an interesting one, for of all the markets he might have chosen to make his point, this is one of the nicest and most tractable of all. Barten and Bettendorf, in their much-admired 1989 paper on estimating demand systems, choose to apply their methods to the price of eight kinds of fish at Belgian seaports over the period 1974–1987. As the authors explain: "Frequently, demand systems are estimated for large aggregates with ill-defined and varying technical characteristics and average prices which are perhaps very partially representative." Fish, on the other hand, provide a nice example of a set of goods with clear and stable characteristics, whose prices are well-defined, market-clearing prices. The product is perishable, so that anticipations of future prices can be ignored, and so on. It would be interesting, in the light of Robbins's remarks, to reestimate the Barten-Bettendorf system with data for the 1990s: how stable will the parameters prove to be?

ally of an extremely weak kind, and they could safely be taken as compelling. Either they were "obviously" true, and verifiable by "introspection," or else they were "obviously" a reasonable approximation to reality. The kinds of assumptions Robbins had in mind in making these claims were those familiar to a beginning student today as the basic assumptions that lead us from elementary consumer and producer theory toward the basic model of supply and demand. Thus, for example, Robbins was happy to postulate that "the individual can arrange their preferences in an order," that "there are more than one factor of production," and so on. Most generalizations of interest can, he feels, be based on such fundamental assumptions, which are compelling, together with some secondary assumptions that must be chosen in a way that is sensitive to the context of the problem at hand (Robbins 1932, chapter 4).

Now if we take this a priori view of the claims of theory, it follows that the task of the empirical worker can amount at best to that of estimating those parameters whose values are unspecified within the theory. If we set aside Robbins's extreme skepticism as to the likely stability of the estimated parameters, we are left with a picture of the relationship between theorizing and statistical analysis that finds an important echo among many economic theorists today, as we will see in chapter 4.

One reason for the pungency with which Robbins expressed his a priorist outlook lay in the fact that he was engaged in a dialogue with an equally extreme opposing view, which dramatically reversed the relative importance of theory and evidence. Robbins's bête noire was the prototypical business-cycle analyst of the 1920s. The view of this group was that statistical regularities existed in macroeconomic data, and these regularities had a considerable degree of stability over time. The best way forward lay in estimating these relationships, in a manner that did not rest on any (dubious) a priori theoretical restrictions whose validity might be questioned. To Robbins, and to other theorists of the 1920s, this approach seemed dubious in the extreme: in the absence of any deep understanding of a stable underlying mechanism that generated these apparent regularities, why should we expect them to show any stability? In fact, the failure of business cycle analysts to predict the collapse of 1929 was seen by Robbins and like-minded theorists as discrediting the entire approach. It was against this background that Robbins wrote his scathing dismissal of the school in *The Nature and Significance of Economic Science*.[3]

While the views of Robbins and those of the business cycle economists formed the two extremes of the debate by the 1930s, many economists took the middle-ground position that had been advocated by Marshall: the best way for-

---

3. Robbins's plea that a priori theorizing would prove a better guide than the business cycle theorists' quest for statistical regularities was not without its ironies. The huge impact of Hayek's LSE lectures of 1931 led Robbins to write down his analysis of the causes of the Great Depression in *The Great Depression* (1934), on the eve of the Keynesian revolution. Robbins later said that this was the only one of his books that he would prefer not to have written (Coase 1994).

ward lay in the careful interplay of theory and evidence. To Marshall, theory alone was empty, while empirical investigations without theory were suspect; only the interweaving of theory and evidence constituted "economics proper" (letter to Edgeworth, 1902).[4] For those who stood in the middle ground, the question was simply one of how best to proceed in confronting theory with evidence. By the late 1940s, two strands of thought would emerge, which, in combination, provided economists with a new and powerful way of doing this.

The Emergence of a Paradigm

Samuelson's *Foundations of Economic Analysis* was first published in 1947, though it had been written a decade earlier. It is a book of great elegance and power. What Samuelson had seen was that the vast bulk of theoretical analyses offered by economists all shared the same elementary formal structure. First came a series of "equilibrium relations" that must hold between certain sets of variables. The system of simultaneous equations defined by these relations pinned down a unique equilibrium outcome. Finally, the impact of any exogenous shock to the system was modeled as a shift in one of the underlying parameters of the model. A comparison of the new equili-

---

4. Whitaker 1996, Letter 713. Marshall was always guarded in his public criticisms of any view, and his letter to Edgeworth is the sharpest statement of his priorities. Edgeworth, on the other hand, pulled no punches in writing of his contempt for the "empirical school" (Sutton 1993).

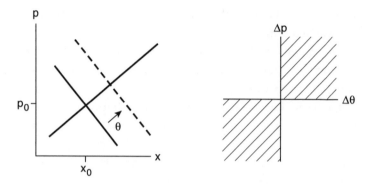

Figure 1.1
The standard paradigm. Left-hand panel: A change in the under-lying parameter θ shifts the equilibrium outcome (x_0, p_0). Right-hand panel: The "empirical content" of the model.

brium outcome with the old provided a prediction for the effect of the shock in question. This was the method of "comparative statics," and the contribution of the *Foundations* was to codify this method, and to unify the major literatures of economics within this framework (figure 1.1). Much of the impact of the *Foundations* came from the unsuspected richness and flexibility of this picture, which provided a vehicle for a surprisingly wide range of familiar and not-so-familiar applications.

It was against the background of these new ideas in theory that Trygve Haavelmo published his classic article on *The Probability Approach in Econometrics*. Published as a 118-page supplement to the July 1944 issue of *Econometrica*, Haavelmo's article confronted the prevailing conventional wisdom, which held that there was no basis for regarding economic data as being the outcome of some probabilistic scheme.

Haavelmo begins by noting that contemporary usage among applied economists favors the application of certain statistics, but that these statistics have no valid interpretation except insofar as they are related to some probabilistic scheme. He then disposes of a popular misunderstanding according to which a probabilistic scheme is only applicable in situations where each observation is an independent draw from the same "population." He points out that the entire set of n observations can be validly interpreted as a single draw ("sample point") taken from an "n-dimensional" *joint* probability law, the existence of which may be purely hypothetical.

Following these prefatory remarks, Haavelmo moves on to his main line of argument. The issue, he explains, is that agents' actions depend in practice on a "great number of factors, many of which cannot be expressed in quantitative terms. What is then the point of trying to associate such behaviour with only a limited set of measurable phenomena, which cannot be more than an incomplete picture ...?" Notwithstanding the complexity of the list of potential influences, however, Haavelmo argues that some actions taken by agents will have systematic and measurable consequences, and it is "only a natural step to attempt an approximate description of behaviouristic parameters."

Then comes a crucial remark: "it is not to be forgotten that the [explanations we offer] are all our own artificial inventions in search of an understanding of real life; they are not hidden truths to be discovered." In making this point, Haavelmo defines what I will refer to as the "weak" or "sophisticated" interpretation of the emerging paradigm, in terms of which the apparatus to be developed is a diagnostic tool to be used in uncovering the working of any systematic mechanisms at work, against a background of complicating influences in a "noisy" world. This leaves open the question of whether there is some "true model" featuring Marshall's sharp distinction between systematic influences and "noise," whose structure we can hope to uncover. (The "strong" interpretation of the paradigm which assumes this is considered in chapter 4.) As to the way in which the tool is to be used, Haavelmo adopts a Marshallian position, quoting Bertrand Russell to the effect that "the actual procedure of science consists of an alternation of observation, hypothesis, experiment and theory." It is the back-and-forth process between theorizing and testing that is the key.

On this understanding, Haavelmo develops a scheme of analysis.[5] At the heart of his discussion is a concern as to

---

5. Haavelmo, like many of the early econometricians, was very interested in time-series investigations of macroeconomic relationships, and many of his examples and illustrations relate to this setting. Most of the modern discussion of methods in econometrics has also focused on this area. In these lectures, I have chosen to emphasise the fundamentally simpler problems that we face in cross-sectional microeconomic studies.

how we can distinguish between apparent regularities that just happen to crop up in some single data set from those regularities whose appearance reflects some underlying law. In the latter case, certain patterns will recur in different data sets between which outcomes will vary in a systematic way only because there are some exogenous factors that differ across data sets.

The aim, says Haavelmo, is to have "theories that, without involving us in direct logical contradictions, state that the observations will *as a rule* cluster in a limited subset of the set of all conceivable observations, while it is still consistent with the theory that an observation falls outside the subset 'now and then.'" The aim of theory, then, is to place constraints on the space of measurable outcomes; but these constraints must be formulated in a way that admits of small and/or occasional exceptions. The role of the probabilistic framework is to allow us to define precisely what is meant by "now and then."

Haavelmo's first substantive concern is with this issue, and he explores it under the heading of "confluent" relationships. The (now obsolete) term "confluent relation" relates to a relationship that remains stable in spite of shifts in the values of endogenous variables within the overall system of simultaneous equations that describe the model. In modern terms, what is at issue here is analogous to looking for the underlying "structural equations" that lie behind the "reduced form relationships" that may be observed in the data.[6]

All this is discussed at a very general level. It is only midway through the article that Haavelmo introduces the notion of separating the observed values of endogenous variables into a "systematic part" and a "disturbance term." Here, for the first time, we meet the notion embedded in Marshall's analogy of the tides: that there are two sharply separable classes of mechanism at work, one yielding large systematic influences captured in the equations of the model, while the other is a secondary influence. To complete the description of the model, as Haavelmo notes, we need to assume some structure for these secondary disturbance terms. The unruly list of potential influences or mechanisms has been partitioned, and

---

6. It is worth noting Haavelmo's rather abstract statement of this point in full, in view of its relationship to the issues explored in chapter 3: "To make this idea more precise, suppose that it be possible to define a *class*, Ω, of *structures*, such that *one member or another* of this class would, approximately, describe economic reality in *any practically conceivable situation*. And suppose that we define some nonnegative *measure* of the 'size' (or of the 'importance' or 'credibility') of any subclass, ω in Ω, including Ω itself, such that, if a subclass contains completely another subclass, the measure of the former is greater than, or at least equal to, that of the latter, and such that the measure of Ω is positive. Now consider a particular subclass (of Ω), containing all those—and only those—structures that satisfy a particular relation 'A'. Let ω_A be this particular subclass. (For example, ω_A might be the subclass of all those structures that satisfy a particular demand function 'A'.) We then say that the relation 'A' is *autonomous* with respect to the subclass of structures ω_A. And we say that 'A' has a *degree* of autonomy which is the greater the larger be the 'size' of ω_A as compared with that of Ω. The principal task of economic theory is to establish such relations as might be expected to possess as high a degree of autonomy as possible."

the secondary (noise) part will now be modeled as a draw, or set of draws, from some distribution.

It will be helpful to begin with the most favorable (i.e., simplest) situation. Suppose the analogy of the tides is accurate, and there is a true model linking an endogenous variable y to a vector $\mathbf{x} = (x_1, \ldots, x_n)$ of exogenous variables, in the sense that

$$y_i = a_1 x_{i,1} + a_2 x_{i,2} + \cdots + a_n x_{i,n} + \eta_i.$$

Here, the index i labels data points, and η_i is a stochastic disturbance term. Now, to obtain good estimates of the coefficients $a_1, a_2, \ldots, a_n$, we need to have a data set in which the values of x_i fluctuate widely, thus leaving a clear trace of x_i's influence on y. In practice, we will work with a limited set of data, and many of the potentially relevant factors may show little variability. The estimated form of the equation may indicate that only a limited subset of the x_i's are significantly different from zero.

Attempts to replicate the results obtained from such a model with new data sets may prove difficult. In the new data set, one of the "insignificant" variables, x_n, may have shifted to a new value, around which it again shows little variability within the (new) data set. Its effect will be to induce a shift in the estimated coefficients $a_1, a_2, \ldots, a_n$, though again a_n remains statistically insignificant.

Now, this might seem a trivial worry, and one that is easily remedied in this simple setup. For all we have to do,

in principle, is to pool the data from our two data sets—
and from further, similar data sets—until we have a
pooled data set within which all the relevant variables
exhibit a sufficiently wide range of (joint) variability, and
we will uncover the true model.

In this simple setting, then, assuming the model of the
tides is a good analogy, we are faced with a merely practical difficulty, which we might hope to circumvent. The
gradual accumulation of data sets, notwithstanding the
apparent inconsistencies in the associated regression estimates, would furnish us with a "grand" data set that
would suffice to lay bare the structure of the "true model."

Once we move beyond the simple setting in which the
tides analogy is valid, however, life becomes much more
difficult. The essence of the tides analogy lies in three
properties, (1) the true model captures a "complete" set of
factors that exert large and systematic influences, (2) all
remaining influences can be treated as a noise component
that can be modeled as a draw from some probability distribution, and (3) the model determines a unique equilibrium. One of the main ideas I want to develop in what
follows, and especially in chapter 3, relates to situations in
which these conditions do not hold: instead of having a
sharp divide between measurable, systematic influences
and factors treatable as noise, I want to consider a setting
in which there are many x_is, some having a larger influence and some a smaller, so that in any finite data set we
will inevitably find that just a few of the x_is are signifi-

cant; nonetheless, whenever we estimate the model, there are always more x_is sitting in the background, which are subsumed in the noise component within the model that we select on the basis of our examination of this particular data set. In other words, I want to take away the sharp distinction between two different types of influence, which we had in the tides analogy, where the astronomical components played the role of the x_is and the meteorological components played the role of the noise component, η_i.

So long as all potential influences are measurable, there is still no problem, in principle. As data sets accumulate, we might reasonably expect to converge bit by bit to a closer approximation to the true model, as all the most important xs reveal their influence. But, in practice, many of the xs may be difficult to measure, even by way of some "proxy" variable that we might use to control for their effects. If this is so, the mere accumulation of data won't help. We are stuck with the fact that some of our systematic influences have slipped into our estimated "residuals," that is, into the noise component.

This problem is not usually regarded as a particularly important one. It is felt that if we can measure the important influences, or at least control for any factors that are hard to measure by including reasonable proxies for their influence, then it is reasonable to model everything else as part of the noise term. The question arises, however, as to whether we should now expect the noise terms, η_i, to have any "nice" statistical properties. If they don't have nice properties, then this is taken as an indication that there may be some influence we have failed to pick up, which is causing the η_i to have some "non-nice" features—and this can be used to motivate a continuing search for a better specification. In other words, the whole idea, in the "sophisticated" approach, is to argue that one reason the η_i might be oddly distributed is that we've left out some systematic influence, so we ought to look further. By the time the η_is are nice, we have probably arrived at the best representation of this data set that is possible on the basis of the available information.

Everything turns on whether we can decide in advance on some desirable list of nice properties. As long as the tides analogy holds, this is not difficult. All we have to do is ask: suppose I have a candidate model of the standard kind, but it differs from the true model, which is also of the standard kind. Then how will this discrepancy manifest itself in the residuals of my fitted regression? Suppose, for example, the true model involves a nonlinear relation between y and x, but I fit a linear model to the data. Then the fingerprint of my failure will lie in the appearance of serially correlated residuals. So one nice property I might ask for is the absence of serial correlation; and so on.[7]

---

7. I have chosen this example advisedly—for among time series econometricians this requirement remains even today a matter of controversy, some econometricians feeling it should be a standard criterion for model selection, while others argue that it should not. So even within the classical paradigm, it is less than obvious what list of nice properties we should ask for.

But what if the tides analogy does not hold? What if there are variables that we cannot measure, proxy, or control for, but which exert a large and systematic influence on outcomes? Then their presence will induce a bias in the estimated coefficients of the model that we fit: were we to impose the "correct" model, with the unobservable variables suppressed, then there is no reason to believe that our fitted residuals would have a nice structure.[8] To use the quest for such nice properties as a basis for model selection may now lead us badly astray.

But Does It Matter?

So how well does the standard paradigm work in practice? Are these difficulties serious? The answer is: sometimes. In those happy situations in which outcomes are driven by a single market mechanism, whose operation is robust enough to override all secondary influences, we may find a clear and sharp pattern emerging in the data, whose interpretation is uncontroverisal (box 1.2). At the other extreme, it may prove very difficult, even in apparently straightforward cases, to uncover some underlying model that accounts for the patterns in the data. Models that appeared to fit for some time may suddenly break down, leading to a search for hitherto unrecognized rele-

---

8. Nor is there any reason to believe that the model we select will correspond to that selected by other researchers, in whose data sets the unobservables may have a different configuration. Put in this way, our problem corresponds exactly to the worries expressed by Haavelmo and his contemporaries as to whether it was realistic to hope that model selection exercises could uncover stable structural relationships.

Box 1.2
From Marshall to Salter

The idea that most economics students are most likely to associate with Marshall is his use of the distinction between "short run" and "long run" to resolve the controversy as to whether price movements were driven by supply and demand, or by the cost of production. His answer was that, in the short run, supply and demand ruled—but in the long run, supply responded to increases in demand, via the entry of new firms or an extension in production capacity. In the long run, prices would fall to reflect any decrease in the unit cost of production made possible by advances in technology.

It was not until the 1950s that large bodies of data became available to test this claim. Modeling the movement of relative prices across different industries involves a number of steps: the different components of unit costs (labor costs, cost of materials, and the equivalent rental cost of capital equipment) need to be analyzed separately, a distinction needs to be drawn between existing (older) capital equipment and newly installed equipment, and so on. A remarkable book published in 1960, by a young British economist, W. E. G. Salter, provided a complete and elegant analysis, in which successive "vintages" of capital equipment embodied lower unit costs of production. Applying this model to British and American data, Salter showed that there was a fairly close correlation between the different components of unit cost,[1] so that labor pro-

---

1. Salter relied on census data, in which labor and materials costs are measured directly. Neither capital costs nor net profits are measured separately, and their sum must be identified with the residual (price minus labor and materials cost).

Box 1.2 (continued)

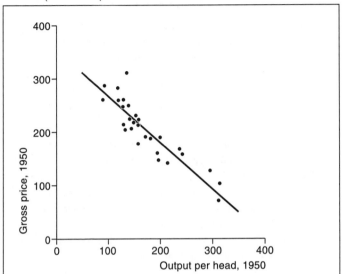

Figure 1.2
Changes in price (vertical axis) versus changes in unit labor costs (horizontal axis) for twenty-eight manufacturing industries in the United Kingdom, 1924–1950 (1924=100). Source: Salter 1960.

ductivity (output per head) served as a good index of the rate of cost decline over a cross section of industries. One of the most striking pictures in Salter's book showed the tight relationship between changes in labor productivity and price across twenty-eight manufacturing industries in the United Kingdom for the period 1924–1950 (figure 1.2).

This correlation, which constitutes only a preliminary step in Salter's extensive study, has been reproduced successfully for various countries. Its consistency at the empirical

Box 1.2 (continued)

level is well established, and its interpretation is generally agreed upon. The empirical results are sufficiently sharp to permit a straightforward analysis of those occasional influences that disturb the relationship, thereby uncovering second-order effects associated, for example, with the adjustment process that follows large and sudden shifts in the pattern of costs.

Salter's book is a classic in the field of Industrial Organization, yet it is little read today, and its findings are rarely cited in textbooks. So clear are these relations, that it seems to be taken for granted that prices follow costs, and that the process of competition ensures that the gains from productivity improvements accrue in the long run to consumers, and not to firms. Yet it would be hard to find a more pithy illustration of the market process at work.[2]

---

2. I wish I could report a happier ending to this story: unfortunately, Salter died at the age of twenty-nine, just three years after the publication of his book, which had won him recognition as one of the profession's most promising newcomers.

---

vant factors (box 1.3). The business of model selection is often a far trickier business than the analogy of the tides might suggest.

Old Worries

These concerns are not new. As the standard paradigm began to take shape from the late 1940s onwards, such methodological worries were voiced by two economists whose views on substantive issues could hardly have been more divergent: John Maynard Keynes and Friedrich von Hayek.

Both Keynes and Hayek expressed grave doubts as to whether the operation of the economy could be captured in a "complete" yet usefully simple model of the kind that Haavelmo and his colleagues had in mind. Both critics focused on the difficulty of "letting the data decide" between candidate models, given the fact that many influences were sporadic in their operation, and others were inherently difficult to measure. On these grounds, both objected to the adequacy of using such a vehicle for testing rival theories. In particular, Keynes took the view that the right way to approach the new econometric methods proposed by Tinbergen for modeling the macroeconomy, was to treat them as a tool for parameter estimation, once the qualitative form of the model had already been chosen on the basis of prior considerations (see endnote 1.1).

Nowadays, these objections are usually seen as misplaced. They are also seen as leading to a rather unconstructive conclusion: if outcomes are heavily influenced by factors whose impact we cannot pin down, or whose size which we cannot measure, then how can we proceed? If we are to judge the case between competing models of how the economy works, then why not let the data decide?

These robust dismissals are indeed justified if the economic world is like the tides. But if the world were as

Box 1.3
A Difficult Case

Does any stable relationship exist between the number of individuals registered as unemployed in any period, and the number of job vacancies advertised in that period? Clearly, the two variables are negatively correlated; good times bring a rise in vacancies and a fall in unemployment. But is the relationship a stable one? If so, what are the factors that determine this relationship? And what economic mechanisms underlie it?

The "u-v relationship," sometimes known as the "Beveridge curve,"[1] has been widely studied by labor economists over the past generation. It is easy to propose particular models in which a stable u-v curve exists. Such models involve workers and jobs that are heterogeneous. Demand fluctuations across firms and industries will generate job losses. A newly unemployed worker may be either a good match or a mismatch for any advertised job. The worker may investigate some given number of possible job opportunities each period and will continue to search over successive periods until a good match is found. A rise in aggregate demand leads to a fall in the flow of people entering unemployment, a rise in the stock of vacancies, and a smaller inflow to fill those vacancies from the reduced stock of the currently unemployed.

---

1. Sir William Beveridge, Director of the London School of Economics from 1919 to 1937, is best known for his pamphlet setting out the aims that were to underpin the postwar expansion of the welfare state. So great was his popular fame in the late 1940s that he once had the happy experience of having a London cabbie refuse his fare; it was an honor, the cabbie told him, to carry such a passenger.

Box 1.3 (continued)

It is clear, however, that matters may be a good deal more complex than this simple story suggests. What, for example, affects the worker's intensity of search? Does this vary with the length of time for which the person has been unemployed, and if so, how? What is the appropriate model for the way in which job severances occur as aggregate demand falls? And so on ...

Empirical investigations of the u-v relationship for the United Kingdom in the 1970s suggested that there was indeed a stable relationship, and that the key shift parameters that fixed its level were those associated with the ratio of unemployment pay to current wage levels, and the hiring and firing costs of firms.

This interpretation seemed to fit British experience between the mid-1960s and the late 1970s: the u-v relationship seemed to have shifted, in the sense that a given level of vacancies was associated with a higher level of unemployment in the 1970s than had been the case in the 1960s. Moreover, this shift seemed to be associated with the introduction in the early 1970s of new regulations that required firms to make payments to workers who were laid off ("redundancy pay"), thereby—the story went—leading to a shakeout of workers before the legislation came into effect, and to a shift thereafter to more cautious hiring policies.

Attempts to fit u-v curves on the basis of such a view led to apparently successful econometric specifications (Gujarati 1972a,b; Taylor 1972). Yet, by the late 1980s, this kind of story seemed unpersuasive. During the 1980s, the "employment protection" legislation that had supposedly led to the shift in the u-v curve was rescinded, yet the curve

Box 1.3 (continued)

remained in the same position it had occupied in the late 1970s. This observation led to a new wave of theorizing, and over the past decade, several alternative interpretations of the observed u-v relationship have been proposed. Some emphasize the distinction between the search behavior of workers who have suffered short-term unemployment and that of the long-term unemployed. (The search behavior of the two groups is different, and their relative numbers shifted during the 1980s.) Other current theories emphasize additional factors that may be relevant: these include, for example, the distinction between vacancies filled by recruiting currently employed workers versus those filled by currently unemployed recruits, and so on.

The *u-v* relationship seems, at first glance, to be one of those simple relations that might form a useful building block within a larger theory of economic fluctuations. Yet pinning down a satisfactory specification of the relationship has proved elusive, at least to date. Whether any stable relationship exists, which can be specified in terms of a small number of "observables," remains an open question.

simple as that, we would long ago have converged to a portfolio of well-founded models. As matters stand, we are still far from such a goal.

One of the most striking disappointments in the research program that grew out of the newly introduced standard paradigm arose in the late 1960s. In the early years of that decade, confidence in the future progress of applied research based on the new paradigm was high; by the early

1970s, however, this confidence had been badly dented. The late 1960s saw the first major challenge to conventional Keynesian views on the modeling of macroeconomic activity; Friedman's early formulation of the monetarist position appeared to be reducible to a set of claims that could be couched very easily within the standard paradigm. Both Keynesians and early monetarists were content to use the same ("IS-LM") framework of equations to describe relationships between the major macroeconomic variables (employment, output, investment, money supply and interest rates). Differences between the two schools, at this point,[9] seem to turn on the size of certain estimated parameters within their common model. Yet research by proponents of both schools failed to resolve these differences. This failure could be blamed on the noisiness of the data. Equivalently, they could be taken as a reflection of the fact that many factors that impinged on the outcomes were absent from the basic model—and controlling for such influences, whose role might be sporadic, and whose measurement might be problematic, would inevitably involve some more or less arbitrary decisions, on which rival researchers were unlikely to agree. A textbook appeal to the standard paradigm was not going to settle the issue.[10]

---

9. Later developments in monetarism, from the early 1970s onward, involved a move away from this framework. For details of these controversies, and the way in which they impinged on economists' views on the testing of theories, see Backhouse 1995.

10. For a discussion of these issues, and of how the later debates between the two schools evolved, see Backhouse 1995, chapter 9.

The Central Theme

I want to argue in this book that the early concerns voiced by such critics as Keynes and Hayek, while they may indeed have been exaggerated, were not misplaced.[11] I believe that much of the difficulty economists have encountered over the past fifty years can be traced to the fact that the economic environments we seek to model are sometimes too messy to be fitted into the mold of a well-behaved, complete model of the standard kind. It is not generally the case that some sharp dividing line separates a set of important systematic influences that we can measure, proxy, or control for, from the many small unsystematic influences that we can bundle into a "noise" term. So when we set out to test economic theories in the framework of the standard paradigm, we face quite serious and deep-seated difficulties. The problem of model selection may be such that the embedded test ends up being inconclusive, or unpersuasive.

My concern, then, lies with the practical difficulties we face in carrying out model selection exercises with a view to testing theories within the framework of the standard paradigm. One way of getting some perspective on these difficulties is to focus attention on extreme settings, in

---

11. In making this point, I would like to distinguish between the view expressed in von Hayek 1989, which emphasized the problems posed by unobservables while maintaining the importance of testability, and the more extreme (and in my view, unconstructive) position sometimes associated with Hayek, which abandons the notion that the merits of rival theories can and should be judged by reference to tests based on observable outcomes.

which model selection is relatively easy, or in which the model selection issue can simply be bypassed.

In chapter 2, I turn to the rare and happy circumstances in which the problem of model selection virtually disappears: here we know—to a good order of approximation, at least—what the true model is. In this setting, economic theory turns out to work remarkably well.

In chapter 3, I turn to the other extreme: here the problem posed by factors that are of substantial importance, but are intrinsically unmeasurable, means that the problem of model selection is so serious as to be intractable. Nonetheless, by relaxing the standard paradigm, and abandoning any quest for a complete model, it turns out that considerable progress can be made in developing a testable theory.

One unfortunate side effect of the dominance of the standard paradigm has been a tendency in some quarters to argue that the only proper kind of model is a complete model of the standard kind; and that the only right way to test a theory is by examining restrictions on regression coefficients within the context of a model-selection exercise. Such views, I will argue in chapters 3 and 4, are overly narrow. In most of the situations that we encounter in economics, the standard paradigm provides our most useful investigative framework. Sometimes, however, it may be more fruitful to work in a looser framework, which avoids any attempt to specify a complete model of the standard kind. Different situations call for different approaches. There is no recipe for research.

2   Some Models That Work

By a model is meant a mathematical construct which, with the addition of certain verbal interpretations, describes observed phenomena. The justification of such a mathematical construct is solely and precisely that it is expected to work.

—John von Neumann

Bachelier's Story

In the year 1900, a young polytechnicien named Pierre Bachelier submitted to the University of Paris one of the most remarkable Ph.D. theses ever written in economics. It was the first of two short theses submitted as part of the candidate's degree requirements, and it ran to a mere sixty-six pages.

Bachelier's thesis is entitled "Theory of Speculation," and it begins by proposing a model for the evolution of stock prices over time. Given today's price, what can we say about tomorrow's price? If we describe tomorrow's price as a random variable, then the expected price tomorrow must coincide with today's price (plus a small correction for the one-day rate of interest); for otherwise, it would be profitable either to buy (or to sell) at today's price, thereby making a positive expected profit on the transaction—and so today's price will rise (or fall) until this condition is satisfied. In other words, stock prices from day to day will follow a "random walk," being equally likely to rise or fall in value (relative to the return obtained on a riskless interest-bearing asset). If we model this kind of process, not in discrete time periods, but in continuous time, then we obtain what is nowadays usually referred to as a "Wiener process".[1] Bachelier's first achievement was to develop the mathematics of this process.[2,3] Armed with these results, Bachelier proceeded to ask the question: how can we place a value on a stock option?

A ("call") option on a stock is a financial instrument that permits its owner to exercise the right to buy a unit of stock at some predetermined price at some future date. If the price of the stock rises to a level exceeding this pre-determined price, then the owner of the option will exer-

---

1. In honor of the MIT mathematician, Norbert Wiener, who studied these processes.

2. Bachelier's thesis predates by five years the paper by Einstein, who independently developed the analysis of such a process and applied it to the modeling of Brownian motion (the movement of small particles in a liquid), thus supplying one of the classic demonstrations of the atomicity of matter.

3. The diffusion equation that defines Bachelier's process admits more than one form of solution. The solution that Bachelier obtained is the only one that satisfies some basic differentiability properties and which has finite mean and variance (See below).

cise this right, and will earn a profit equal to the difference between the stock's actual price and the exercise price at which he or she is allowed to buy it. (A "put" option works the other way around, allowing the holder to sell at some predetermined price. These options will be exercised if the stock price is sufficiently low.) In what follows, we simplify by assuming away the payment of dividends during the period when the option is held.

Now, the value of such an option will clearly depend upon the volatility of the stock price. Intuitively, what we are looking at is the weight in the tails of the probability distribution of the stock price at some future date (figure 2.1).

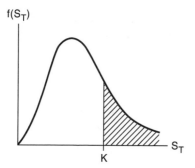

Figure 2.1
The probability density function $f(S_T)$ of the stock price at time $t = T$, given the price at time $t = 0$. The exercise price, or "strike price," labeled K, is the price above which the option will be exercised. Our focus of interest lies in the weight of the tail of the distribution, as indicated by the shaded area.

Bachelier assumed, implicitly, that the agents in the market were risk neutral. The value at time $t = 0$ of a (European call) option, could then simply be expressed

$$C = e^{-rT}E(\max(S_T - K, 0)), \tag{1}$$

where the random variable S_T denotes the stock price at the expiration date $t = T$, K is the exercise price, and r is the rate of interest (discount rate).

Now Bachelier's solution indicated that S_T could be described by a normal distribution whose standard deviation increased proportionally with the square root of T, viz.

$$\sigma = a\sqrt{T}.$$

So, to value the option, subject to this model of the evolution of prices, we need to pin down the value of a. This can be estimated, albeit crudely, by calculating the standard deviation of the "day to day" changes in the stock price over some period in the recent past. By doing this, Bachelier was able to calculate predicted values for options on French government bonds. He was also able to predict the probabilities that these options would be exercised. In both cases, his predicted values conformed closely to the actual prices observed, and to the fraction of options exercised.

Bachelier's thesis did not impress his examiners. The custom was to award a thesis one of two grades (*avec mérite*, and *avec grand mérite*). The higher grade was, in practice, essential if the candidate was to obtain a university teaching post. Bachelier's passed *avec mérite*, and he made no further contribution to economics. To contemporary economists, the problem was perhaps too far removed from their usual interests. To mathematicians, the analysis was not sufficiently rigorous. Yet Bachelier's thesis anticipated one of the most fruitful literatures in economics by half a century. It was not until the 1960s that economists would turn to these issues and retrace Bachelier's footsteps.

Option Pricing Today

To calculate an option price, we must first decide on some true model that describes the evolution of the stock price; second, we need to estimate a number that measures the degree of volatility in the stock price; and finally, we need a formula that allows us to calculate, given the true model, the price of the option as a function of the estimated volatility parameter.

Modern treatments of the problem model the evolution of the underlying stock price using a lognormal, rather than a normal distribution:[4] writing the current price as S_0, the

---

4. Consider a random variable X, defined on $0 < X < \infty$, such that $Y = \ln X$ is normally distributed with mean μ and variance σ^2. Then X is lognormally distributed, with parameters μ and σ^2, its distribution function being written $\Lambda(x|\mu, \sigma^2) = \text{Prob}\{X \leq x\}$. The associated density function is given by

$$d\Lambda(x) = \frac{1}{x\sigma\sqrt{2\pi}} \exp\left\{-\frac{1}{2\sigma^2}(\ln x - \mu)^2\right\} dx \qquad (x > 0). \tag{2}$$

ratio S_T/S_0 is described by a normal distribution with mean μT and variance $\sigma^2 T$.

The centerpiece of the modern theory lies in moving from Bachelier's restrictive setting of risk-neutral agents, where equation (1) holds, to the more general setting in which agents may be risk averse (Black and Scholes 1973; Merton 1973; Cox, Ross, and Rubinstein 1979). A full treatment is beyond the scope of this chapter; for an introductory account, see for example Gemill 1993. The point of departure involves a simple idea; We consider an investor who buys Δ units of stock, and sells 1 unit of the option, where the value of Δ is chosen so that the gain he makes from a rise in the price of the stock is exactly offset by the loss he incurs in his ("short") holding of the option. In other words, he forms a portfolio that yields a constant return, independently of the movement of the stock price. (As p

---

The j-th moment of the distribution is given by

$$\lambda'_j = \int_0^\infty x^j \, d\Lambda(x) = \int_{-\infty}^{+\infty} e^{jy} \, dN(y) = e^{j\mu + \frac{1}{2}j^2\sigma^2}.$$

In particular, the mean of the distribution equals $\exp(\mu + \frac{1}{2}\sigma^2)$. The j-th moment distribution is defined by

$$\Lambda_j(x|\mu,\sigma^2) = \frac{1}{\lambda'_j} \int_0^x u^j \, d\Lambda(u|\mu,\sigma^2). \tag{3}$$

Two nice properties of the lognormal distribution are, (i) if X is lognormal with parameters μ and σ^2, then $1/X$ is lognormal with parameters $-\mu$ and σ^2, (ii) the j-th moment distribution function can be expressed in terms of the distribution function itself: a direct calculation (Aitcheson and Brown 1966, p. 12) yields

$$\Lambda_j(x|\mu,\sigma^2) = \Lambda(x|\mu + j\sigma^2, \sigma^2).$$

(These formulae hold for all j; the special case where j is a positive integer is of special interest, as the λ_j are then the ordinary moments.)

changes, Δ must be changed too, in order to maintain this property.) This portfolio, being risk free, will command a price that coincides with its expected value—irrespective of investors' attitudes to risk. It turns out that, building on this insight, it is possible to develop the "Black-Scholes" formula, which gives the value of the option as a function of the initial stock price S_0, the exercise price K, and the variance parameter σ, together with the interest rate r and the time to exercise T.

While this formula looks complex at first glance, it is in fact no more than an explicit form of equation (1), where the probability distribution of the stock price at time T is lognormal and the mean return on the stock coincides with the rate of interest r (risk neutrality); see box 2.1. In a risk-neutral world, then, matters are relatively simple. The deep result is that this formula continues to hold good in a setting where agents are risk averse. (For a discussion, see for example Hull 1989.)

How Well Does It Work?

Bachelier's data is illustrated in figure 2.2. It suggests that the basic model that he developed worked remarkably well in predicting option prices for French government securities on the Paris Bourse in the closing years of the nineteenth century.[5] The modern empirical literature,

---

5. Bachelier's formula defines a relationship between the exercise price K and the price of the option C, for a given date of exercise T. So, for a given T, we could test this by looking at the predicted value of C given K, or at the predicted value of K given C. Bachelier uses the latter procedure (figure 2.2).

Box 2.1
From Bachelier to Black-Scholes

To go from formula (1) of the text to the Black-Scholes formula, we need to invoke a couple of basic properties of the lognormal distribution (footnote 4, properties (i) and (ii)). Denoting by S_T the stock price at time T, K the exercise price, T the time to maturity, and r the discount rate, we have

$$C = e^{-rT} E(\max(S_T - K, 0)). \tag{1}$$

To ease notation, we normalize by writing the current stock price S_0 as unity, so we measure everything "per \$1 worth of current stock." The random variable $S_T/S_0 \equiv S_T$ is described by a lognormal distribution with parameters μT and $\sigma^2 T$. It follows that the random variable $s = 1/S_T$ is lognormal with parameters $-\mu T$ and $\sigma^2 T$ (property (i)), so (1) can be written as

$$e^{rT} C = E\left(\max\left(\frac{1}{s} - K, 0\right)\right),$$

where s has distribution function $\Lambda(-\mu T, \sigma^2 T)$, whence

$$
\begin{aligned}
e^{rT} C &= \int_0^{1/K} \left(\frac{1}{s} - K\right) d\Lambda(s \,|\, -\mu T, \sigma^2 T) \\
&= \int_0^{1/K} \frac{1}{s} \, d\Lambda(s \,|\, -\mu T, \sigma^2 T) - K \int_0^{1/K} d\Lambda(s \,|\, -\mu T, \sigma^2 T) \\
&= \lambda'_{-1} \Lambda_{-1}\left(\frac{1}{K} \,\middle|\, -\mu T, \sigma^2 T\right) - K\Lambda\left(\frac{1}{K} \,\middle|\, -\mu T, \sigma^2 T\right),
\end{aligned}
$$

where $\lambda'_{-1} = e^{\mu T + \frac{1}{2}\sigma^2 T}$. Under risk neutrality, the mean return $\mu + \frac{1}{2}\sigma^2$ must coincide with the rate of interest r, and invoking property (ii), footnote 4, this becomes

Box 2.1 (continued)

$$= e^{rT} \Lambda \left(\frac{1}{K} \,\middle|\, -\mu T - \sigma^2 T, \sigma^2 T \right) - K\Lambda \left(\frac{1}{K} \,\middle|\, -\mu T, \sigma^2 T \right)$$

$$= e^{rT} N \left(\ell n \frac{1}{K} \,\middle|\, -\mu T - \sigma^2 T, \sigma^2 T \right) - KN \left(\ell n \frac{1}{K} \,\middle|\, -\mu T, \sigma^2 T \right)$$

$$= e^{rT} N \left(\frac{\ell n \frac{1}{K} + \mu T + \sigma^2 T}{\sigma \sqrt{T}} \,\middle|\, 0,1 \right) - KN \left(\frac{\ell n \frac{1}{K} + \mu T}{\sigma \sqrt{T}} \,\middle|\, 0,1 \right).$$

Writing the standard normal distribution $N(x|0,1)$ as $N(x)$ to ease notation, multiplying across by e^{-rT} and once again invoking the "risk neutrality" equation, we have

$$C = N \left(\frac{\ell n \frac{1}{K} + r + \frac{1}{2}\sigma^2 T}{\sigma \sqrt{T}} \right) - Ke^{-rT} N \left(\frac{\ell n \frac{1}{K} + rT - \frac{1}{2}\sigma^2 T}{\sigma \sqrt{T}} \right).$$

This coincides with the Black-Scholes theorem, when the initial price S_0 is written as unity.

which is based on the Black-Scholes model, has focused heavily on problems surrounding the measurement of σ. The easiest approach here is the one followed by Bachelier, which involves estimating the standard deviations of period-to-period changes in the stock price over some recent period (20 weeks, say).[6] An alternative method can be used in cases where there are several different options (of different durations, say) on each stock. Here we can use the observed price of one option to infer a value of

---

6. See, for example, Black and Scholes 1973, Finnerty 1978.

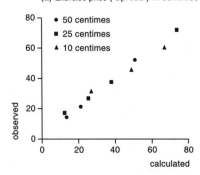

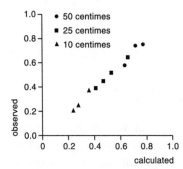

Figure 2.2
Bachelier's results. Panel (a) shows the observed exercise price
versus the predicted exercise price (each measured relative to the
futures price) for options of different prices (50, 25, and 10 cen-
times). Panel (b) relates to the predicted probability of exercise.

σ, and then use this to predict the values of the other options.[7] Studies that use such indirect methods to infer a value of σ generally achieve somewhat better predictions of option prices.

A deeper issue surrounds the validity of the underlying model of stock price movements. It is generally agreed that the conventional model, according to which the (log) stock price T periods hence is described by a normally distributed random variable with mean 0 and standard deviation $\sigma\sqrt{T}$ provides a good approximation to empirical data. It is also agreed, however, that it fails systematically in one respect: the frequency with which very large (positive or negative) changes are observed is somewhat greater than that predicted on the basis of this conventional model. The effect of placing greater weight in the tails of the distribution is that the Black-Scholes formula will slightly undervalue call options whose exercise price is far above the current price.[8] Practitioners make a small adjustment for this on a rule of thumb basis. For the theorist, however, it poses an important potential challenge to the conventional model.

---

7. A more usual procedure is to combine information on all options to obtain a "best estimate" of σ, and then apply this to obtain estimates of individual option prices. See, for example, Latané and Rendleman 1976.

8. It will also undervalue put options whose exercise price is far below the current price. The empirical evidence presented by Black and Scholes 1973 suggests however, that the model tends to overprice (resp. underprice) options with high (resp. low) standard deviation estimates, and they suggest that this may be attributable to an error-in-variables problem (Whaley 1982, p. 33).

There are two views on this: some researchers feel that empirical departures from the conventional model should be addressed, not by abandoning the assumption of lognormality, but by modifying the description of the underlying stochastic process. Others, following Mandelbrot, argue that the selection of the particular solution to Bachelier's equation is justified only by arbitrarily imposing the ad hoc restriction of "finite mean and variance." If we set aside this restriction, we admit a broader set of solutions, and the lognormal distribution is replaced by the family of "stable distributions," and in particular by the Pareto-Levy distribution, which has "fatter tails" than the normal. (On this issue, see Mandelbrot 1964. On recent developments in modeling, see Mandelbrot 1997, chapters E1 and E6.)

What is of interest here, relative to the agenda of the present lecture, is that we are dealing with a situation in which the true model—the underlying model of stock price movements—is known to a degree of precision adequate for the purpose in hand. Debates focus on the choice between two alternative model specifications whose empirical properties differ in ways that will have a small effect on predicted option prices. The only parameter that needs to be estimated empirically is the volatility parameter that we can easily measure to a fair approximation, so that debate centers on the choice of alternative estimation procedures for this parameter that may enhance the accuracy of measurement. In terms of the standard paradigm, this is as good as things get. We have reasonably close agreement on an underlying true model that is known both to the agents in the market and to the economist whose concern lies in testing the theory. Moreover, the predictions of the theory work well, and debates are directed not at questioning the correctness of the theory, but on the fine-tuning of the underlying description of the true model.

In the next section, we turn to a problem that lies in a quite different area of economics. Once again, however, we find ourselves in a setting where there is little difficulty in writing down a representation of the true model that is known both to the agents in the market and to the observing economist.

Understanding Auctions

During the past ten years, the study of auctions has attracted an unusual degree of interest among applied game theorists. One reason for this lies in the fact that, in an auction, the rules of the game are specified explicitly, so we are very close to knowing the true model of the situation. It is not fully known, however, since we do not usually know the value that each bidder places on the item, nor is this information available to rival bidders. Many of the practical difficulties with obtaining testable predictions from auction theory derive from the fact that we are forced to uncover this information indirectly, by looking at the pattern of bids—a point to which I will return. For the moment, however, I'd like to look at a setting in which problems of this kind are minimized: a setting in which oil companies bid for exploration and drilling rights over offshore oil tracts.

The geography of offshore oil drilling is illustrated in figure 2.3, which shows a typical "tract map." The value of drilling rights on any particular tract will be the same for any firm. This value, however, is not known prior to drilling. Rights are auctioned tract by tract, and since the oil-field extends over an unknown area, a firm that is already operating in a given tract will be in a much better position to estimate the profitability of operating in an adjacent tract. In the setting we are looking at, we distinguish two kinds of bidder: those already operating on a tract adjacent to the tract being auctioned (the "informed" bidders) and those not operating on an adjacent tract (the "uninformed" bidders).

With this setting in mind, consider the problem faced by a single informed bidder—who knows, let's say, the true profitability of the tract, when bidding against a number of rivals who do not know the true value, but who must instead guess its value by reference to the known profitability of remote but roughly similar sites.[9] For these rivals, armed with inferior information, is it not best to stay out of the auction, and leave the field to the informed bidder? Will they not find, in the face of such competition,

9. This setup was analyzed by Wilson (1967), Weverbergh (1974), and Engelbrecht-Wiggans, Milgrom, and Weber (1983).

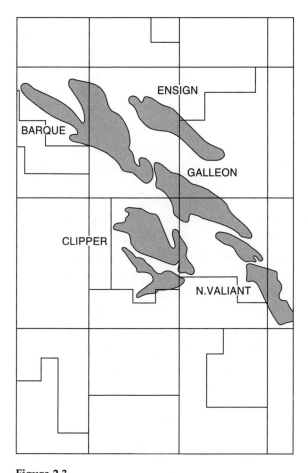

Figure 2.3
A tract map of the Sole Pitfield, which lies off the coast of the
United Kingdom. Shaded areas indicate named deposits in which
wells are operating. The horizontal and vertical lines mark tract
boundaries.

that they win the tract only in the unfavorable situation where its value is low, and lose it when its value is high?

The central implication of a game-theoretic analysis of this situation is that this is not the case: what we will observe is that the uninformed agents do bid—but that they achieve an average profit (payoff) of zero from this activity. Notwithstanding the unprofitability of their endeavors, we cannot have a situation in which they opt out and take no part in the bidding.

This may seem paradoxical, but the reasoning that leads to this conclusion offers a nice illustration of an "equilibrium" argument: were the uninformed agents to opt out, then the best bidding strategy for the informed player is to bid low (close to zero, or—more generally—close to the auctioneer's reservation price). But if the informed bidder follows this strategy, then it now becomes profitable for any one of the uninformed agents to make a slightly higher bid. So we can't have an equilibrium in which the uninformed players are inactive.

If we follow through this intuitive line of argument, we can see how a game-theoretic analysis of this situation must lead to a number of predictions (box 2.2). To test these predictions, we need to have access to data on the true profitability of each tract, following the exploitation of that tract. We also need to know, tract by tract, who the bidders were. Finally, we need to know which if any of these bidders was currently working in an adjacent tract (and who is therefore identified as an informed bidder).

The predictions relate to the average ex post profitability of different groups of tracts, where the classification is made on the basis of whether or not the (single) informed bidder did or did not bid for the site in question.[10]

The model predicts:

1. The average profit of uninformed firms over all tracts equals zero; the average profit of informed firms over all tracts is strictly positive.

2. Consider the tracts on which the winning bid was made by an uninformed player. Split these tracts into two groups: (a) those on which the informed player made a bid, and (b) those on which the informed player did not make a bid.

Then: the average profitability of the (a) tracts is strictly positive, while the average profitability of the (b) tracts is strictly negative.

The results reported by Hendricks and Porter 1988 are shown in table 2.1. The pattern of profitability is as predicted. This example is widely regarded as one of the nicest applications of a game-theoretic model in the literature. Relative to our present concerns, it illustrates the power of this kind of analysis in situations where the structure of the game is known to all agents, as well as to the observing economist.

---

10. In practice, there might be many informed bidders. Hendricks and Porter 1987 postulate that, in this case, the informed bidders will cooperate rather than compete. If so, the "one informed-bidder" model is still valid. Their examination of the evidence is consistent with this interpretation.

Box 2.2
An Auction Game

Consider a game involving two bidders, one of whom knows the true value, v, while the other knows only that v has been drawn randomly from some probability distribution, which for the sake of the illustration, we take to be uniform on the support $[0, 1]$.

A pure strategy for the uninformed player is simply a bid, viz. a number between 0 and 1. A mixed strategy involves drawing a bid p from some probability distribution defined over the domain $0 \leq p \leq 1$. The uninformed player uses a mixed strategy at equilibrium, his bid being described by a random draw from a distribution whose probability density function is denoted $g(p)$.[1] The informed player, who knows v, uses a pure strategy, which takes the form of a rule specifying his bid s as a function of v, that is, a bid function $s(v)$.

We will show that the following strategies form a Nash equilibrium, that is, neither player can improve on his expected payoff by using any other strategy, given the strategy of his rival:

Strategy of Uninformed Player: Choose p as a random draw from the uniform distribution

$$g(p) = 2 \quad \text{on } \left[0, \tfrac{1}{2}\right].$$

Strategy of Informed Player: Bid half the true value, that is,

---

1. It is easy to see that the uninformed player must "mix" in any equilibrium—for if there is an equilibrium in which he plays a pure strategy p, the informed player will, for any known value $v > 0$, find it optimal either not to bid (when $v \leq p$) or to bid just above p (when $v > p$). So the uninformed player only wins when $v < p$, and this strategy is inferior to a strategy of never bidding.

Box 2.2 (continued)

$s(v) = v/2$ for $0 \le v \le 1$.

To show that these strategies form a Nash equilibrium, we need to show that neither player can improve on his payoff, given his rival's strategy. For the uninformed player, who is using a mixed strategy, this requires that every p in the support of the strategy (that is, every p between 0 and $\frac{1}{2}$) yields the same expected payoff, and that this payoff cannot be bettered by not bidding (which yields payoff zero) or by bidding any p outside this support. Since a bid of $p = \frac{1}{2}$ wins with probability one, given the strategy of the informed player, the uninformed player certainly can't do better with a bid of $p > \frac{1}{2}$. We now show that any bid in the range $0 \le p \le \frac{1}{2}$ yields an expected payoff of zero, whence the optimality of the uninformed player's strategy follows. This can be seen from figure 2.4, which identifies for a given p the ranges of v over which (a) the informed player's bid of $\frac{1}{2}v$ wins; (b) the uninformed player's bid of p wins, and since $v > p$, he makes a profit of $v - p$, and (c) the uninformed player's bid of p wins, and since $v < p$, he makes a loss of $p - v$. It is clear from the diagram, given the uniform distribution of v over the range $[0, 1]$, that the expected payoff to the uninformed player is zero.

It follows that the uninformed player is indeed using an optimal reply; no choice of p, or distribution over choices of p, can yield a strictly positive profit.

We now turn to the informed player. Given v, he bids $s = v/2$, and his probability of winning with this bid, given that the rival bid of p is uniformly distributed on $\left[0, \frac{1}{2}\right]$ is $2s$ (figure 2.5). His profit, if he wins, equals $v - s$. Hence his expected profit is simply $2s(v - s)$. This function takes its maximum at the point $s = v/2$, as is easily checked by dif-

Box 2.2 (continued)

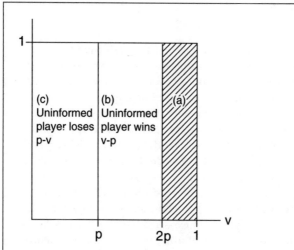

Figure 2.4
The figure shows, for a given bid p by the uninformed player, how his payoff varies with the true value v. In zone (a), shown shaded, the informed player wins and the uninformed player receives zero. In zones (b) and (c), the uninformed player receives payoff $v - p$, which may be either positive—zone (b)—or negative—zone (c).

ferentiating. This confirms the optimality of the informed agent's strategy.

An easy extension of this result, which is of importance empirically, is to let the support of v include negative values, so that for some $x > 0$, we have $-x \leq v \leq 1$. This allows for the fact that some tracts are unprofitable. The informed player will not, at equilibrium, bid on these tracts. The uninformed player, who still makes zero profit

Box 2.2 (continued)

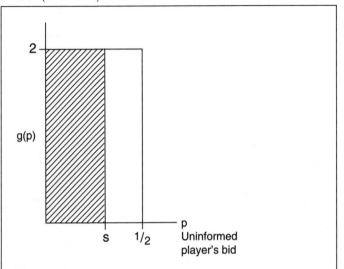

Figure 2.5
The shaded area equals the probability that the informed player wins, with a bid of s, $0 \leq s \leq \frac{1}{2}$, given that the uninformed player's bid p is uniformly distributed on the interval $[0, \frac{1}{2}]$.

overall, makes strictly negative profit on bids for these tracts. We take advantage of the presence of tracts of this kind when splitting the sample of outcomes in empirical testing (table 2.1).

Table 2.1

Average net profit earned on tracts of different categories. Source: Hendricks and Porter 1988.

Category of tract	Mean net profit	Standard deviation of sample mean
Informed bidder wins	6.76	3.02
Uninformed bidder wins	−0.42	1.76
Uninformed bidder wins, and informed bidder bids	0.78	2.64
Uninformed bidder wins, and informed bidder doesn't bid	−2.69	0.86

The rules of the auction pin down the model here, subject only to one prior restriction, which is tested directly: this says that when there are two (or more) informed agents, they behave cooperatively, so that the pattern of bids, and of profitability, is the same as that which holds in the "one informed agent" model.

Extensions

The study of auctions has advanced rapidly over the past decade. The theory has found some striking practical applications: the recent bidding scheme for transmission rights for the radio spectrum in the United States were designed by Preston McAfee, Paul Milgrom, and Robert Wilson, on the basis of a quite sophisticated game-theoretic analysis (Milgrom 1998).

At the level of testing theory, the main problem facing researchers is that, once we move beyond some rather special situations, the predictions hinge upon such factors as the beliefs of bidders, regarding, for example, the valuation placed upon the object being auctioned by rival bidders. A comprehensive analytical survey by Laffont 1997 discusses the extent to which testable predictions can be developed, which depend on directly observable outcomes; this review serves inter alia to underline the fact that the example we looked at in the preceding section is rather special. Over the general run of situations we encounter in practice, such straightforward predictions are not available. Rather, the method of analysis lies in a model-selection exercise designed to uncover the bidding rules used by the agents on the basis of their observed bids. Any testing of theory must be carried out jointly with this model-selection exercise.

Summing Up

My claim in this chapter has been that in those occasional but happy circumstances where the underlying model can be (more or less) determined a priori, the track record of economic models is quite impressive; here the headaches posed by the model-selection process are minimal. The situations to which I turn in chapter 3 constitute the opposite extreme; here the problems posed by "unobservables" become so serious that we cannot hope to list all those factors that may exert large and systematic influences on outcomes.

These situations involve a search for generalizations that will hold good across a range of different markets, thus leading to predictions that can be tested by looking at a cross-section of industries—a central aim in the field of Industrial Organization. Now, when we look at the general run of industries, we are struck at once by the fact that every industry has some unique features. Many features that may exert a significant influence on market outcomes may be very difficult to measure, proxy, or control for in a cross-industry study. If we attempted to write down some general economic model that contained a full list of parameters sufficient to control for all economically relevant market characteristics, we would face a daunting task.

To what extent can we hope, then, to generalize? Are there any mechanisms that operate robustly across some interestingly broad class of markets, in a way that overrides the unique features of particular markets? If the answer is no, then there is little scope for the kind of general claims that (I.O.) economists like to advance about the functioning of markets.

But if some robust mechanisms do exist, which work in a similar way across disparate industries, how are we to model their operation? If we despair of writing down a true model, in which all systematic influences are explicitly represented, then how can we proceed? The metaphor of the tides is not going to be very helpful here; perhaps what we need is a new metaphor.

3 Relaxing the Paradigm

In studying Darwin ... I have arranged his methods as a sequence of different strategies in the face of decreasing information.

—Stephen Jay Gould

Carnot's Story

In the year 1828, a short book of 118 pages was published in Paris, which would, after a lapse of many years, lay the foundations of classical thermodynamics. Its author, Sadi Carnot, was a young and virtually unknown French engineer. Carnot's book was concerned with one of the most pressing engineering problems of the age: what factors determined the efficiency of operation of a steam engine?

It was the age of steam. Britain's industrial leadership had been built upon steam technology, and advances in the design of steam engines would continue to set the pace of industrial advance for two more generations. Rival designs for engines were many and various; Cardwell

1989 (p. 73) lists no less than seven fundamentally different principles of operation that had been used in early heat engines. Any notion of a "typical" or "normal" type of engine was untenable. What was evident to all, however, was that Watt's design, which set the pace in the late eighteenth century, had been surpassed by a new generation of machines developed in the Cornish mining industry, following the early work of Trevithick and culminating in the now leading design of Woolf.

Books and articles on the subject proliferated. The favored style of these contributions was heavily mathematical, and authors who aimed to make some impact among engineers followed Guyonneau de Pambours 1835, 1839, in developing a model that involved an explicit representation of all relevant features of a specific engine. By incorporating empirically measured parameters into the model, de Pambours could produce a prediction of the efficiency achievable by a specific engine (see endnote 3.1).

Carnot's approach was different in the extreme. Instead of building a "realistic" mathematical representation of some typical engine, he began with a different question. He asked: is there anything that can be said, independently of the details of design, about the factors that must ultimately limit the efficiency achievable by *any* engine?

With this question in mind, Carnot reduced the description of the engine to a simple abstract representation, in an attempt to isolate some basic features common to a large class of engines. He then asked: is there anything that can be said as to the maximum operating efficiency of any engine that has these features? Armed with this simple representation, Carnot was able to establish a bound on the operating efficiency of any engine of a particular kind (box 3.1).

The reception given to these new ideas was one of polite reviews, followed by silence. The gulf between Carnot's abstraction and the usual form of contemporary theoretical discussion was vast; the sheer "unrealism" of the analysis was enough to consign it to oblivion. Carnot's ideal engine used a gas; it was familiar to all engineers that steam engines, in which the processes of expansion and compression were accompanied by a process of condensation, outperformed the "air" engines that matched Carnot's abstraction. As to the idea of two heat sources, while Watt's design had used two cylinders, one of which was a condenser (a design that conformed more or less to Carnot's abstract picture), the most efficient design of Carnot's day, due to Woolf, had dispensed with the condenser, making the relation of Woolf's engine to Carnot's picture seem remote in the extreme. When challenged by engineers to give some predictions arising from his theory, Carnot pointed to the implication that operating at high pressure would lead to greater efficiency. His audience was unimpressed; to practical engineers, who had hit on this idea on the basis of experimental investigations some years earlier, this was old news. It was not until 1850, when Clausius restated and publicized Carnot's ideas, that they

Box 3.1
Carnot's Argument

Carnot began with the notion that the essential principle of operation of the engine lay in the fact that a certain quantity of heat ("caloric") fell through a certain range of temperature.[1] Reduced to its essence, he felt that an ideal engine would involve no more than a cylinder and piston moving through a cycle of four steps (figure 3.1).

In step (i), the piston moves out from A to B, allowing the gas to expand, while the cylinder is in contact with a source of heat, which maintains it at a constant temperature T_1. In step (ii), the piston continues to move out but now the heat source is removed: the system is isolated, in the sense that it neither loses nor gains any heat. During this step, the temperature of the gas in the cylinder will fall

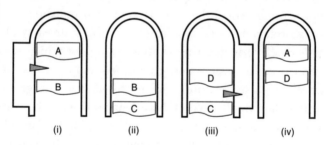

Figure 3.1
The Carnot Cycle. The four phases involve (i) expansion at a constant temperature (A → B), (ii) expansion while thermally isolated (B → C), (iii) compression at a constant temperature (C → D), (iv) compression while thermally isolated. Source: Atkins 1984, p. 18.

1. On Carnot's theory of heat, see endnote 3.2.

Box 3.1 (continued)

to, say, T_2. In the last two steps of the cycle, the piston moves back in: during step (iii), the cylinder is in contact with a heat source that maintains the gas at a constant temperature of T_2. In step (iv), the cylinder is once again isolated, and the temperature of the gas now rises. At the end of the cycle, the piston is back in its starting position, and the temperature has returned to T_1.

This four-step cycle through which the engine moves can be illustrated on a diagram that shows the pressure and volume of the gas at each point. As we move through the cycle, a locus is traced out in pressure-volume space, as shown in figure 3.2. It can be shown that the area enclosed

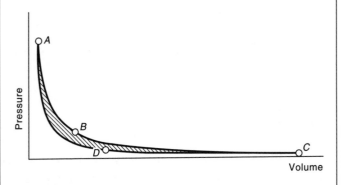

Figure 3.2
The work supplied by the engine is proportional to the area within the locus traced out in pressure-volume space over the course of a cycle. The states labeled (A–D) correspond to the states indicated in figure 3.1. Source: Atkins 1984, p. 18.

Box 3.1 (continued)

by this locus provides a measure of the work generated by the engine (see, for example, Atkins 1984, p. 18 ff.). Moreover, any engine of the class considered by Carnot will trace out a similar locus in pressure-volume space, but the area enclosed by that locus cannot exceed the area generated by Carnot's idealized engine. This is what leads to the idea of placing a bound on the efficiency of operation of all engines of a particular class.[2] Carnot's bound is very simple: the fraction of heat energy that is converted to work equals $(T_1 - T_2)/T_1$.

2. The class of engines considered by Carnot are not, as it happens, very efficient. A similar diagram for a class of engines of modern design will be found, for example, in Atkins 1987, p. 93.

took hold.[1] Carnot, alas, had died in the meantime, a victim of the cholera epidemic of 1832.

Back to Economics

Markets, like steam engines, are many and various. A full description of all the large and systematic influences on outcomes, even within a single market, may be impossibly long and messy. Yet, in some circumstances, we may bypass the problem of attaining a complete description of all influences and simply focus directly on whether any

1. Carnot's analysis is now seen as marking the beginning of classical thermodynamics (see Atkins 1987).

general principles apply over some broad class of markets, irrespective of the detailed differences that arise from one of these markets to the next.

In what follows, I turn to a classic problem in the field of Industrial Organization: the problem of explaining market structure.

Why are some industries dominated, even at the global level, by a handful of firms? What determines the level of market concentration (as measured, say, by the market share of the top firm, or the top handful of firms)? Are there economic mechanisms that force the level of concentration in some industries to be very high, or is it just the accidents of history that have made particular industries develop in this way or that?

One reason for the deep and continuing interest that economists have devoted to this and related questions in the field of market structure, is that this area of economics is particularly rich in apparent statistical regularities, which link the level of market concentration to variables such as the advertising/sales ratio of the industry, the level of R&D intensity, the strength of scale economies, and so on. That such regularities appear in data sets that span different industries, which vary hugely in many characteristics that we cannot hope to control for, suggests that some very strong and robust mechanisms are at work here. A major goal of research in this area is to uncover the natural description of what is driving such apparent regularities, in the hope of thereby obtaining indirect evidence on the workings of the competitive mechanisms that are molding these patterns in the data.

Getting Started

An easy model to start from is a simple two-stage game. In the first stage, firms make various irreversible decisions that involve the outlay of sunk cost (for example, the firms enter the market by building a production plant; carry out R&D to reduce unit costs ("process innovation") or to enhance the technical characteristics of the product ("product innovation"); spend on advertising to build up a brand image, and so on). In the second stage of the game, we take as given the firms' unit costs of production and the consumers' willingness to pay for the offerings of each firm, and we consider some form of price competition taking place among firms.[2]

A simple example that will serve to introduce some key ideas is provided by the elementary Cournot model. Here the only decision made at stage 1 by each of the firms

2. Technically, by analyzing a (Nash) equilibrium of this second-stage (sub)game, we work out the profit of each firm. We can then backtrack to analyze the first stage of the game. Here we define the game by using the "solved-out" profit function of the second-stage subgame to define the payoff function, which specifies each firm's payoff (second-stage profit minus sunk outlays incurred at stage one) as a function of its own strategy and the strategies of its rivals. This procedure amounts to computing a subgame perfect equilibrium of the two-stage game.

(potential entrants) is to enter or not enter. The N firms that enter will, in the second stage of the game, sell a homogenous good produced at constant marginal cost to a population of consumers, whose combined demand for the good is specified as a strictly decreasing function $Q(p)$, where p denotes price. The strategy of each firm is simply to choose an output level, given the output level chosen by its rivals. Market price is specified as that corresponding to the total output produced. An increase in the number of entrants causes price to fall toward marginal cost, and the profit earned by each firm in the second stage of the game to fall toward zero. The equilibrium number of entrants in this two-stage game is the largest integer N, such that each firm's second-stage profit covers the fixed cost of entry $\varepsilon > 0$.

Now suppose we increase the size of the market, by replicating the population of consumers, so that the market demand schedule $Q(p)$ is replaced by $SQ(p)$, where S is a measure of market size. Then a rise in S implies a rise in the number of firms entering the market at equilibrium. If we measure concentration by the ("one-firm sales concentration ratio") $C_1 = 1/N$, then as $S \to \infty$, $C_1 \to 0$. This is the simplest example of a "limit theorem" or "convergence theorem"; it states that concentration falls to zero as the size of the market increases (figure 3.3, panel (a)).

Now, if we try to apply this simple idea to some empirical data, we immediately encounter two problems that lead directly to the heart of the matter. The first of these relates

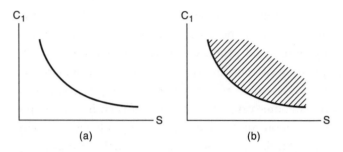

Figure 3.3
Market size, S, and concentration, C_1, in (a) the Cournot example, and (b) the class of "exogenous sunk cost" models.

to the way in which we have modeled the second stage of the game. The representation of firms' strategies as a once-and-for-all choice of the quantity of output is clearly unrealistic. Firms, in practice, are free to set different prices, or produce different levels of output, in different periods, and they may choose to do so in fairly complicated ways, as they react to the prices or output levels set by their rivals in earlier periods. It is difficult to say very much in general about the form that price competition will take. This, however, is the lesser of our two problems.

The model we have looked at so far is one in which firms offer homogenous products. In practice, firms' products will differ from one another in terms of various attributes (geographic location, product characterization, etc.). Once we introduce models with differentiated products, it turns out that in analyzing the entry stage of the game, we find that multiple equilibria are endemic. There may be equilibria in which a small number of firms each produce

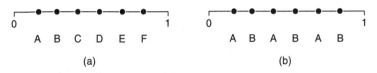

Figure 3.4
In Hotelling's "simple location game," each firm introduces production plants at one or more locations on a line segment. Entering at any location involves a cost of 1. The payoff to any plant is given by the length of the line segment, consisting of points (consumers) closer to it than to any rival, multiplied by S, a measure of market size. Equilibrium outcomes in this game depend heavily on the way in which we allow firms to enter (simultaneously, sequentially, etc.) and will typically involve both "fragmented" equilibria, where many firms each operate at a single location (panel (a)), and "concentrated" equilibria, where a smaller number of firms each operates at more than one location (panel (b)).

at several geographic locations, or offer several distinct product varieties, while there are other equilibria in which a large number of firms each produce at only one location, or offer a single product variety (figure 3.4). One consequence of this is that the relationship between S and C_1 now takes the form of a lower bound (figure 3.3(b)): for a given S, there is a *lowest* value of C_1 that can be attained, but we cannot exclude the appearance of other equilibria in which C_1 lies above this level.[3]

---

3. The kind of indeterminacy, illustrated in figures 3.3(b) and 3.4, relates to the appearance of multiple equilibria in models where firms offer differentiated products. This is just one example of a phenomenon that is endemic throughout the literature on market structure. For practical examples of mechanisms that can lead to a delicate dependence of outcomes on the details of the entry process, see, for example, Sutton 1991,

One thing that will crucially influence the outcome, in this setting, is the way in which firms enter the market, and the way in which each firm conditions (or does not condition) its product-entry decisions on rivals' decisions. In other words, the simple two-stage game that we introduced earlier is too primitive to allow for the kinds of complex interactions that may occur as successive firms enter the market and introduce new production plants or product designs. But what would a realistic representation in terms of some multistage game look like? It is in grappling with this issue that we arrive at the point where the search for a true model becomes futile. The problem is that there are many "reasonable" models, and to choose one over another we would have to have access to knowledge about various subtle features of the entry process, such as the belief that each firm had regarding the way in which its choice of location would or would not affect its rivals' decision making. To cut through this kind of difficulty, it seems appropriate to drop any notion of the true model, and to work instead in the less restrictive setting of a class of models.

Beyond the Standard Paradigm: A Bounds Approach

Rather than specify any particular form of entry process, we begin with a general class of multistage games, con-

---

chapter 6. For cases involving other mechanisms that again lead to the dependence of outcomes on features of the model that are notoriously difficult to measure, proxy, or control for, see Sutton 1998, chapters 14 and 15.

sisting of $T + 1$ stages. Each firm is assigned some stage, labeled t, that defines its date of arrival in the market. At any stage from t to T inclusive, the firm may take actions. An action involves making one or more discrete and irreversible investment. An investment results in the entry of a product at some location in an abstract space of locations.[4]

This framework allows a wide menu of entry games: these range from cases where all firms are assigned the same arrival date ("strategic symmetry") to cases in which some firms that arrive late will condition their actions on the actions already taken by early entrants.

By stage T, all investments are complete. We can now summarize the outcome of the investment process by describing the configuration of products owned by each firm in the abstract space of locations. In the final stage of the game, some form of price competition occurs, and we summarize this stage by writing down a profit function that defines the profit of each firm as a function of its own set of products, as well as the set of products owned by

4. While this setup clearly includes location games (figure 3.4), it is sufficiently abstract to encompass many other kinds of model that have been used in the literature on market structure. For example, in a game where firms choose plants of different production capacities, an action amounts to picking a real number denoting the plant's capacity. In models where each firm chooses some number of product varieties to offer, but in which all varieties are treated in a symmetric manner, we can represent a firm's action by an integer; and so on. (The details of these constructions are described in Sutton 1998, chapter 2.)

each of its rivals.[5] By making appropriate assumptions on the form of this profit function, we can begin to draw some conclusions about the form that market structure may take.

The key idea is this: irrespective of how we design the entry process, it is easy to show that all (pure strategy perfect Nash) equilibria satisfy two properties:

1. No firm has a portfolio of product varieties (locations) on which it makes an overall loss ("viability").

2. There is no gap left in the market, in the sense that, given the locations of all products entered by all firms, there is no (set of) products that can be added by a new entrant, from which it can earn a strictly positive profit ("stability").

We proceed by defining a configuration satisfying these two properties as an "equilibrium configuration."[6] No

---

5. It is conventional to maintain two (empirically reasonable) assumptions regarding cost and demand: (1) firms operate subject to constant marginal costs, and (2) an increase in market size is modeled as a replication of the population of consumers (i.e., the distribution of consumer tastes is unaffected). This implies that, as market size increases, demand schedules shift outward in a simple proportionate manner. An immediate consequence of these two assumptions is that equilibrium prices are independent of market size S, and so we can write a firm's profit, or sales revenue, in the final stage subgame in the form $S\pi(\cdot)$, or $Sy(\cdot)$, where the arguments of the profit or revenue function specify the number of firms that have entered, and their respective products.

6. It is worth noting that our search for results that hold independently of the form of the entry process has led us to a form of "bounded rationality" (see box 3.2).

matter how we design the entry process, the resulting game has a set of pure strategy Nash equilibrium outcomes that lie inside the set of equilibrium configurations.

Market Structure Revisited

What can be said about the relation between industry characteristics and market structure at this level of generality? One immediate result is that we can now recast the preceding analysis of exogenous sunk cost models in general terms. The lower bound to concentration illustrated in figure 3.3(b) now emerges as an immediate consequence of the viability condition. A key feature of this lower bound is that it converges to zero as market size increases: the level of concentration may fall to arbitrarily low levels in a sufficiently large economy. This convergence property provides a point of reference against which we can explore the distinctive way in which market structure evolves in those industries in which advertising and/or R&D competition plays a significant role. The idea, stated loosely, is as follows:

If it is possible to enhance consumers' willingness-to-pay for a given product to some minimal degree by way of a proportionate increase in fixed cost (with either no increase or only a small increase in unit variable costs), then the industry will not converge to a fragmented structure, however large the market becomes.

To capture this idea, we imagine that a firm, instead of paying a fixed fee of ε to enter and produce a product, is instead free to spend some fixed outlay Fu^β in order to produce a product of quality u, where u is an index of consumers' willingness-to-pay for the firm's product. (We can think of u as a measure of technical performance, or brand image, etc.) Consider a firm offering product quality v, in the presence of rivals offering products whose qualities are $(u_1, u_2, \ldots, u_n)$, will earn a profit denoted $S\pi(v \mid u_1, \ldots, u_n)$. We will be particularly interested in a situation where an entrant leapfrogs all existing firms in terms of their R&D outlays, in the sense that it offers a product of quality $k\bar{u}$, where $\bar{u}$ denotes the highest quality level offered by any existing firm. Suppose that such fixed outlays are effective in raising the willingness-to-pay of at least some given positive fraction of all consumers. Then, if we choose some suitably large value of k, we will be able to guarantee the firm some minimal level of final-stage profit *independently* of how many low-spending rivals it faces.[7] Moreover, the profit it earns will rise in proportion to the size of the market; explicitly, we suppose that, associated with any $k > 1$, there is a constant $a > 0$, such that the profit of this high-spending entrant is at least equal to aSy, where Sy denotes the preentry level of industry sales. It can be shown that, under these circumstances, there exists a lower bound to the level of concentration C_1 that can be supported in any equilibrium configuration—irrespective of

---

7. The idea is this: the entire burden of quality improvement has fallen on fixed, as opposed to variable costs. Even if rivals' prices fall to marginal cost, our deviant high-spending firm still enjoys a strictly positive price-cost margin, and this guarantees some minimal level of profit.

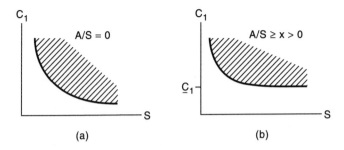

Figure 3.5
A "nonconvergence" result. In panel (a), a rise in market size may lead to an indefinite fall in the one-firm concentration ratio C_1. In panel (b), no matter how large the size of the market S, the one-firm concentration ratio C_1 cannot fall below the lower bound $\underline{C}_1$ in any equilibrium configuration.

the size of the market S (box 3.3). This result constitutes a simple 'nonconvergence theorem', according to which the possibility that market structure becomes increasingly fragmented as the size of the market increases breaks down (Shaked and Sutton 1987; figure 3.5).

The intuition underlying this nonconvergence result turns on the interplay between the viability condition and the stability condition. If we consider a configuration in which all firms have very small market shares, then the viability condition ensures that the revenue of each firm, relative to S, is small. Hence its fixed outlays $F(v)$ must also be small, relative to S. But if $F(v)$ is small, then so, too, is the fixed outlay that an entrant must incur in leapfrogging to a higher quality level, thereby capturing a high market share

Box 3.2
Rationality

In the preface, I remarked on two "beginner's questions."
One asked, "Do agents really maximize?," while the other
asked, "How can you hope to capture the messy complexity of the real world in some simple mathematical model?"
In pursuing the second of these questions, we have arrived
at the class-of-models approach. In so doing, we encounter
the first question, for once we follow a class-of-models
approach, we automatically abandon the need to insist
upon strict profit-maximizing behavior. The reason is as
follows: if we want to judge, on the basis of the data,
whether an agent has taken a maximizing decision, we
need to know the "true model" within which the agent
was working. Suppose, for example, that we wanted to
judge whether some firm had used a profit maximizing
strategy in deciding how many products to introduce, or
where to introduce these products. To evaluate its decision, we would have to know, for example, when the
firm entered, relative to its rivals; for the firm, in making
its decision, will have to decide on whether and how
its actions will affect future actions of its rivals. Without
knowing the details of the entry process, we will not in
general be able to decide on the basis of observable outcomes (the number and locations of each firm's offerings in
product space) whether or not the firm chose a profit maximizing action. An action that is optimal within a "simultaneous entry" model will not in general be optimal if we
change the entry process to one of "sequential entry." So
instead of posing the intractable question, Do agents really
maximize? it may be more fruitful to ask, to what extent
can we deduce, by reference to observed actions, whether
the agents were maximizing? In a setting where we do not

Box 3.2 (continued)

know, and cannot identify, a true model that can be assumed to be common knowledge to agents, the most we can hope to do is to identify some subset of actions as being inconsistent with maximization within any admissable model. What we are led to, along this route, is a form of "bounded rationality."

In the setting considered here, this amounts to a replacement of the profit maximizing behavior assumed in the usual Nash equilibrium setup with the viability and stability conditions that define the set of equilibrium configurations. If we knew the particular form of the entry game, we could look for a Nash equilibrium within that game. What this would require, in addition to viability and stability, would be that each product occupies an optimal location, given the location strategies followed by the firm's rivals. But without knowing the form of the entry game, we cannot specify these strategies, and we cannot therefore impose this additional requirement.

Finally, it is worth remarking that, in imposing the viability and stability conditions, all that we require of *all* agents is that they do not violate the viability condition. For the stability condition to be satisfied, what we require is that there is no unexploited profit opportunity. If any such opportunity arises, then *some* agent will fill it: there is always one smart agent available who will fill the gap in the market. There is an analogy here with the arbitrage argument used in the finance area (chapter 2), where again we do not need *all* agents to be maximizers.

and so a level of profit that is also high relative to S. A formal statement of the result is given in box 3.3.[8]

This theorem begins from the notion that we can identify some pair of numbers, a and k, which measure the effectiveness of jumping to a high-spending strategy. The numbers a and k, however, are not directly observable. Before we can move to an empirical test, a second theorem is needed, which restates the nonconvergence theorem in terms of directly observable quantities. The intuition underlying this theorem is straightforward: the parameter β measures the effectivess of fixed outlays in raising consumers' willingness-to-pay for improvements in perceived quality. If β is large, such spending is ineffective, and the ratio of such outlays to industry sales will be low. Here, too, our lower bound $a(k)/k^\beta$ will be low. On the other hand, where β is

---

8. To some readers, it may seem at this point that we have almost jettisoned the "game-theoretic" content of these models, in moving to these two simple principles. It is worth emphasizing that this appeal to the stability and viability conditions retains, and indeed crystallizes, the distinctive contribution of game-theoretic models to the market structure literature. This contribution lies in shifting the analysis away from the enumeration of different special features of the pattern of technology and tastes in the industry, towards asking a simple, and quintessentially game-theoretic question. To understand why some industries are concentrated, we ask: why can these industries not support a fragmented structure, with many small firms? The answer is that there must be some "profitable deviation" that would become available to some firm, were such a fragmented structure to prevail. In other words, if the fragmented structure satisfies the viability condition, then it must violate the stability condition (see box 3.3). Following this line of argument, we arrive at conclusions quite at odds with those familiar from the earlier literature (See, for example, the remarks in Sutton 1998 on the topic of increasing returns to R&D).

low, indicating that such spending is effective, the fixed outlays will be higher as a proportion of industry sales revenue, and the lower bound to concentration will also be higher. (While this result is intuitive, a proof is lengthy; the details will be found in Sutton 1998, chapter 3.)

One way of testing this prediction is by examining the relation between concentration and market size for two sets of industries, a control group in which advertising and R&D play no significant role, and an experimental group in which the ratios of advertising and/or R&D expenditure to industry sales revenue exceed some (arbitrary) threshold value. An example, taken from Sutton 1991, is shown in figure 3.6.[9] Statistical estimation of the implied lower bound for the scatters shown in these figures confirms the prediction of nonconvergence in the latter group of industries. Independent studies by Robinson and Chiang 1996 and by Lyons and Matraves 1996 confirm this result.[10]

This example constitutes the simplest illustration of the bounds approach to market structure. For a fuller discussion of the approach, including its application to R&D–intensive industries, and to the size distribution of firms, the reader is referred to Sutton 1998.

---

9. In testing such predictions, it is customary to work with a four-firm (or five-firm) concentration ratio, since confidentiality requirements preclude publications of C_1 in official statistics.

10. See also Lyons, Matraves, and Moffat 1998. The econometric techniques appropriate for bounds estimation are discussed in Sutton 1991, chapter 5.

Box 3.3

A Nonconvergence Theorem

Suppose that, of a large[1] number N_0 of potential entrants, some number $N < N_0$ have entered. The outcome of the investment process may be expressed as a configuration of qualities $(u_1, u_2, \ldots u_N)$, where u_i denotes the quality level of firm i. We denote the highest level of quality attained by any firm as $\bar{u}$. The fixed cost of attaining quality level u is written in the form $F(u) = F_0 u^\beta$, where $\beta > 0$ is a constant.[2]

Suppose there exists some constant $k > 1$, and an associated constant $a(k) > 0$, such that a firm offering quality $k\bar{u}$, in the presence of (any number of) rivals whose qualities are no greater than $\bar{u}$, achieves a profit level of at least $a(k)Sy$, where Sy denotes total industry sales prior to entry. We will then be able to place a lower bound on the maximal market share (i.e. the one-firm sales concentration ratio) that must hold in any equilibrium configuration.

To see this, denote the one-firm sales concentration ratio as C_1, and note that, by definition, no firm can have sales revenue exceeding $C_1 Sy$. It follows from the viability condition that it cannot incur a level of fixed outlays exceeding this value, whence $F(\bar{u}) \leq C_1 Sy$.

Now consider a firm that has not entered in this configuration. Suppose it deviates by entering with quality level $k\bar{u}$. It incurs a fixed outlay of $F(k\bar{u}) = k^\beta F(\bar{u})$, and its profit is at least equal to $a(k)Sy$. The stability condition requires that such an entrant does not achieve a positive profit,

---

1. In the sense that if all N_0 firms enter, we will violate the viability condition.
2. We can always choose to label the quality index so that $F(u)$ can be expressed in this way.

Box 3.2 (continued)

whence it follows that

$a(k)Sy < k^{\beta}F(\bar{u}) \le k^{\beta}C_1 Sy$

whence we have

$C_1 \ge a(k)/k^{\beta}.$

This provides a lower bound to concentration. (In fact, we can do a little better than this, by choosing the "best" value of k in order to make our lower bound as high as possible.)

The Standard Paradigm Reconsidered

What would happen if, instead of pursuing the above question by looking for a bound in the data, we had instead approached the question by way of the standard paradigm? The earlier literature on the subject did exactly this: the idea was to investigate the "causes of concentration" by positing a regression relationship between some measure of concentration and a set of "explanatory variables" that included, in our present notation, both S/ε (or its reciprocal) and the advertising-sales ratio A/S. Now if the theory set out above is right, so that the data is correctly represented by figure 3.5, then such a regression is a misspecification. It is, however, an easy exercise in econometric theory to predict, subject to the present theory, the result of running such a regression on the pooled sample that includes both industry groups: we will find that S/ε will appear with a negative sign, while A/S is expected to

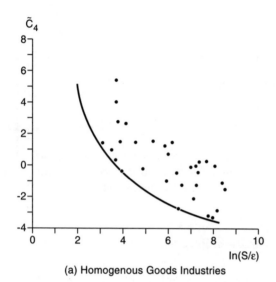

(a) Homogenous Goods Industries

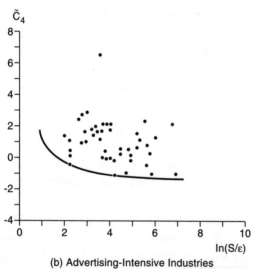

(b) Advertising-Intensive Industries

carry a positive coefficient, because it picks up a weak "intergroup" effect (Sutton 1991, p. 127). So the present characterization encompasses the rather fuzzy results that were obtained in the past by imposing a standard regression model.

So, what is wrong with just imposing the standard paradigm, and regressing concentration on some set of explanatory variables? Apart from the fact that the regression approach, in this instance, is difficult to motivate on the basis of a satisfactory theoretical model (Sutton 1991, chapter 1) there are two compelling arguments. The first emerges once we go beyond the relatively easy exercise examined above, towards more challenging problems. Take, for example, the relationship between R&D intensity and concentration—the most investigated question in the older, regression-based literature. Attempts to fit regression results through a rather diffuse cloud of observations

Figure 3.6
Testing the nonconvergence theorem. The figures show data for two groups of industries, all of which are in the food and drink sector, for six countries. Panel (a) shows a control group for which advertising spending is less than 1% of industry sales revenue. Panel (b) shows the corresponding results for those industries where the advertising-sales ratio exceeds 1%. The vertical axis shows a (logit transformation of the) four-firm concentration ratio $\tilde{C}_4 = \ell n(C_4/(1 - C_4))$. The horizontal axis shows (the log of) market size, measured by the ratio of total industry sales revenue, S, to the minimum efficient size of plant in the industry, ε. Source: Sutton 1991.

led to no consensus among researchers as to the form of
the relationship, or even as to whether any systematic relationship existed (see Cohen and Levin 1989 for a review).
Using a bounds approach, on the other hand, we arrive at
a clear and sharp characterization (for details, see Sutton
1998, part 1).

The second argument is statistical in nature: the standard
paradigm rests on the notion that there is some deterministic theoretical model that pins down the "central tendency" in the data. The fingerprint we look for in this
setting is a nice symmetric (possibly normal) distribution
of residuals about the fitted regression line. If, however, the
natural representation of the patterns in the data relates to
the presence of a bound, then what we expect to see in the
data is a nonsymmetric distribution, in which residuals[11]
are distributed in a skew fashion, with a bunching of values
in the region close to the bound. This is the pattern that
typically appears when we look at residuals in this area; for
an example of this, see Sutton 1998, page 302. This suggests
that, even on narrowly statistical grounds, a bounds representation offers a more natural description of the data.

Summing Up

My aim in this chapter has been to show that, even in an
area where writing down a complete model seems a

---

11. In figure 3.6, the distance between an observed value of C_1 and the
lower bound to C_1 at the appropriate value of S.

daunting task, it may nonetheless be possible to bypass this problem, while nonetheless developing a theory that generates testable predictions. Such a line of attack does not preclude the idea of aiming at a complete theory in the manner of the standard paradigm. What such a quest would involve would be to augment the simple viability and stability principles with additional assumptions, which might be tailored to different subgroups of industries, in order to place tighter restrictions on outcomes than those derived here. While some limited progress of this kind is possible (see Sutton 1991, chapter 9), it remains an open question as to how far we can hope to go. The bounds approach should not be seen as an alternative to the standard paradigm, but as complementary to it. It is best seen as offering a point of comparison against which we can assess the incremental explanatory power of more highly structured theories.

It might seem, at this point, that this kind of strategy would be of wide applicability. Unfortunately, its scope is likely to be fairly limited. What is special about the market structure problem is that we can identify certain arguments that are extremely robust to changes in the details of the underlying models, and which place a (lower) bound on outcomes. In other words, all the complicating factors that are hard to measure, proxy, or control for—at least in cross-industry studies—happen to operate in the same direction, pushing concentration levels above our lower bound.[12] This leaves us with a nice statistical

---

12. The analogy with Carnot's steam engines is again evident here.

description of the data, in terms of a "one-sided error distribution."

In most cases, the unobservables for which we cannot control will not be so easily handled. This may not rule out the use of a class-of-models approach—but it will probably make it harder to implement successfully.

In these last two chapters, I have been exploring the boundaries of the standard paradigm. But the vast bulk of economic research lies in the middle ground between these extremes, and in that middle ground, the standard paradigm provides us with the best investigative tool we have. It is time to return to Marshall . . .

4   Testing

Dalton combined singleness of mind with a strong preference for clear-cut explanations ... he liked his conceptual models to be clearly understandable, and when he was wrong ... he was clearly wrong; he did not try to confuse issues by sheltering behind face-saving clauses, ambiguous pronouncements and other sophistries.

—D. S. L. Cardwell, *From Watt to Clausius: The Rise of Thermodynamics in the Early Industrial Age*

San Diego Revisited

As San Diego's taxicab industry moved to a free-entry policy from 1978 onward, the number of licenced taxicabs more than doubled from its 1978 figure of 410, reaching 928 by 1984. As the problem of oversupply developed, one response that suggested itself to the authorities was to decontrol prices: why not let the forces of supply and demand equilibrate the market? In a situation of oversupply, the argument went, prices will fall, and exit will follow, until market equilibrium is restored. The city council began the process of price deregulation by redefining the fixed rate as a ceiling, before moving to full deregulation in 1980. Far from resolving the problem, the freeing of prices merely compounded the difficulties.

The reason is not hard to see: the elementary competitive model of supply and demand is the wrong model here, for one of its key assumptions is that consumers enjoy full information on rival firms' prices. For the taxicab market, this is rarely a good assumption. In the case of San Diego, where 40 percent of all cab rides are taken by visitors as opposed to residents, it is badly wrong. The appropriate model for this market is one that distinguishes two groups of consumers, "informed" and "uninformed." In this model, equilibrium involves the appearance of two groups of sellers, one offering a higher price and capturing a share of the tourist trade, while the other offers a low price and enjoys a higher volume of business, capturing both part of the undiscriminating tourist business, and (almost) all of the residents' market (For a "two-price" model of this kind, see Salop and Stiglitz 1977).

During the early 1980s, a two-price equilibrium developed in San Diego. Some cab companies focused on price-sensitive residents by offering fares lower than the $2.50 per mile that had been the ceiling up to 1980, while some introduced a fixed fare of $10 in addition to $2.50 per mile, concentrating their business on the airport and on major tourist attractions.[1] Throughout the 1980s, the authorities went through a series of policy changes in their attempts to curb the high-fare strategy, introducing initially a new ceiling based on average measured fares plus 20 percent. Meanwhile, excess supply problems at the airport were compounded as local residents shopped the line, refusing the first cab in line, and waiting until a low-price cab arrived (Lupro 1993).

The failure of price deregulation to resolve the problems of oversupply led airport authorities to impose their own curbs. In the early 1980s, they capped the number of taxis that were allowed to operate from the airport at 450; later, they further restricted supply by splitting these cabs into two groups, allowing the two groups to operate on alternate days. By the mid-1980s, there were three groups, each allowed to work the airport only one day in three. Finally, in 1991, price regulation was reimposed at the airport, with the authorities fixing a standard rate per mile.

No subtle econometric techniques are needed to see that supply and demand is the wrong model for airport taxicabs: the qualitative features that emerge in this story are

---

1. San Diego's experience of a two-price equilibrium was relatively mild. The most dramatic example I have encountered occurred at Stockholm airport following the deregulation of the 1990s: taxi firms split into two groups, with the high-price group charging about three times the fare level of the low-price group. The former group gained no business from the locals, but earned a good living from unsuspecting tourists.

enough to justify the alternative model of imperfectly informed consumers. In this respect, the taxicab example affords a nice illustration of the kind of evidence that is often most persuasive in economics: two rival models are distinguished by sharply different qualitative predictions.

The evidence that leads to major shifts of view in the profession is often of a simple qualitative kind. The early debate between Keynesians and monetarists, as I noted in chapter 1, proved difficult to resolve by appealing to econometric studies built on the *IS-LM* framework. What tilted the balance in this debate at the end of the 1960s was not evidence of this kind, but the appearance of high unemployment coinciding with high inflation. It was this ugly fact, and not any more formal kind of evidence, that was decisive in shifting the terms of the debate from the early 1970s onward.[2] Simple qualitative observations may sometimes provide the most powerful evidence against a strongly held theoretical position.

Such situations are, however, the exception. Usually, to discriminate between the predictions of rival theories, we have no alternative but to plunge into a rather subtle analysis, hunting for patterns in the data that may favor one interpretation over another.

---

2. Ironically, what this observation contradicted was not Keynes's macroeconomics; rather, it contradicted a generation of conventional wisdom that had grown up in Keynesian circles, building upon the early "Phillips curve" research, according to which a more or less stable trade-off existed between unemployment and inflation.

Back to Marshall ...

We saw in the first lecture that the theory program championed by Marshall and Edgeworth, and crystallized by Robbins, was developed in reaction to the research program of the empirical school. The driving force of this latter program lay in the search for patterns in the data, especially in the field of business-cycle research. The danger in such a program is that apparent regularities may show little stability over time, or across different markets. Patterns can mislead. In contrast to this empirical program, the theorists aimed to begin by postulating a few simple assumptions that could be justified on an a priori basis by reference to introspection. But would these few assumptions generate testable predictions? And would it be possible in practice to carry out the appropriate tests?

The development of the standard paradigm appeared to give a clear and consistent set of answers to such questions: the core assumptions we begin from would usually need to be augmented by some secondary assumptions in order to complete the model. The model's predictions would then be tested jointly with a model-selection or parameter-estimation exercise. Tests on coefficient restrictions implied by the theory would then allow the theory to be rejected. All this seems clear enough; but in practice matters are more difficult. The pitfalls involved in "letting the data decide" between alternative specifications are serious, even in relatively favorable settings (Leamer 1983).

As we saw in chapter 1, the presence of factors that shift occasionally, and so exert only a sporadic effect on outcomes, makes model selection more difficult: the presence of systematic influences that we cannot measure, proxy, or control for makes matters even worse.

Now, the bulk of empirical work in economics is not concerned with theory testing as such. Rather, such work is investigative in nature. The aim is to try out fitting some model with a view to uncovering the mechanisms that are driving outcomes in some particular data set. A to-and-fro process may develop between such investigations and the development of theoretical models. But suppose, whether through such a process or otherwise, we have a clear and well-motivated theory, and we aim to ask whether the theory's predictions work? Then where do we stand? When we set out to test a theory jointly with a model-selection exercise, what is at stake?

When Predictions Fail

Suppose, first, that the theory fails. There are two lines of response. We can always appeal to the idea that we have now realized the relevance—in this data set—of some factor for which we have not controlled. Such responses merely serve to underline the fact that the world is more unruly than Marshall's analogy of the tides would suggest—there are always lots of potentially relevant factors. Still, this problem is not all that serious, for if every researcher needs to appeal to some such fix, the theory will lose credibility anyway; after repeated rescues, we will finally conclude that the theory is wrong. The interesting question at this point is: what do we abandon? By far the most likely response is to abandon some of the secondary or ancillary assumptions that were added to obtain a complete model of the standard kind. It is unlikely that the researcher will question certain core assumptions about which he has strong priors[3].

There is nothing intrinsically wrong with holding strong priors; every continuing research program is built upon some set of maintained assumptions (box 4.1). The point I would like to make here is that the business of testing one theory against another does not follow any simple prescription. We looked in chapter 1 at the business of model selection by reference to a search for a model whose residuals had nice statistical properties; I noted that there was no agreed set of nice properties on which all researchers would agree. In this chapter, where my concern is with the testing of theories jointly with a model-selection exercise, the judgmental element is rendered all the greater by the fact that different researchers will hold different priors regarding some core elements of the theory.

3. There is nothing surprising in this: as Lakatos emphasized long ago, every discipline has some core of basic assumptions. Ideally, the status of these core assumptions will be secured by the indirect evidence supplied by their repeated use as building blocks in theories that have succeeded.

Box 4.1
Strong Priors

Suppose we are engaged in modeling demand in a setting where a complex array of product characteristics affect the sales volume of each product. Say we find the coefficient on the price variable to be positive. What do we do? Many if not most researchers would conclude that some relevant factor had been omitted, and would search for candidates. Here getting a negative sign on the price variable has become one of the criteria of model selection; the fact that demand curves are downward sloping is not treated as part of the set of testable predictions of the theory under investigation. This example is uncontroversial, since the prior in question here is one that all researchers will share. But what if we push the argument to priors shared by most but not all economists?

Modeling Aggregate Consumption

Early research on the consumption function, which links aggregate consumer spending to national income, indicated a sharp difference between short-run and long-run behavior. In the short run, consumption responds only weakly to changes in current income, but over long periods of time, the ratio of aggregate consumption to national income remains fairly steady. An early analysis by Duesenberry (1949) proposed that a kind of "ratchet effect" was in operation, as spending habits adjusted slowly to long-run changes in income. A more elegant solution, in the same spirit, was set out in Milton Friedman's classic *A Theory of the Consumption Function* in 1957. The new theory

Box 4.1 (continued)

was quintessentially neoclassical in form; it posited a consumer who maximized lifetime utility by using each period's observation of current income to revise his estimate of future income; the level of current consumption was then chosen in the light of this revised income calculation. Thus an unexpected windfall in income in the current period would raise consumption only by a modest amount, while a permanent upward shift would generate a correspondingly larger rise in consumption. This core prediction of the theory was tested using a natural experiment based on veteran's windfall receipts to ex-wartime prisoners who received unanticipated reparation payments (see Mayer 1972). The evidence suggested a higher propensity to consume out of these windfall receipts than could easily be accounted for on the basis of the theory. Moreover, the empirical fit to time-series data obtained by Friedman was less good than he obtained using the rival, "habit persistence," model of Duesenberry. Nonetheless, it was the permanent income hypothesis (together with the closely related life cycle hypothesis) that came to be regarded as the standard model of aggregate consumption behavior. The rival Duesenberry theory suffered primarily from its lack of a theoretical underpinning in individual maximizing behavior, rather than any shortcomings at the empirical level (Gilbert 1991, section 7).

Later Developments

The most important innovation in the literature following Friedman's contribution began with the work of Hall

Box 4.1 (continued)

(1978), in which the permanent income model was coupled with the idea that consumers forecast income on the basis of a rational expectations model. Extended in this way, the theory generated some striking predictions.

The implications on which Hall focused related to the idea that, once consumers form a rational expectation of future income movements, the proportionate change in consumption in any period will have zero covariance with variables in the lagged information set—a prediction that was broadly supported by the data. A second implication, however, was that—if we make reasonable assumptions about the movement of aggregate income over time—the theory does *not* imply the basic fact that has motivated the modern literature on the subject: that aggregate consumption is less variable over time than is income. To reconcile the model with this basic fact would require strong and implausible restrictions on the income-generation process (Gilbert 1991, p. 15).

The rational expectations/permanent income hypothesis thus seems to be falsified empirically. Should we simply conclude that the theory is wrong, and that some quite different alternative theories should be explored? Or should we attempt to modify some secondary features of the model in order to reconcile the theory with the observed facts?

Here reasonable researchers will take different views. Recent developments in the theory have considered the role of liquidity constraints, the presence of some consumers whose savings behavior is driven by habit formation, and the role of a precautionary motive for saving, in the light of

Box 4.1 (continued)

uncertainty about future income (for a review, see Deaton 1992). In spite of the richness of avenues studied, however, there appears to be a consensus among a majority of researchers in the area that the two basic ideas in the theory are right, at least in some approximate sense: the long-run, average level of consumer spending follows some kind of permanent-income level, and consumers respond differently to anticipated versus unanticipated changes in income. These ideas appear, for most researchers, to be strongly held priors, and they carry over in some form to most of the more recent models.

As I noted in the text, there is nothing intrinsically wrong with holding strong priors in favor of certain ideas: all research programs will embody some basic ideas that are maintained throughout. Yet there is an obvious danger here, too: an incorrect theory might be defended indefinitely in the face of mounting counterevidence. The best corrective to this danger is offset by the presence of competing research program. The most important alternative approach in this area is that initiated by Davidson, Hendry, Sraba, and Yeo (1978). Here the idea is to place only very weak theoretical restrictions on the consumption-income relationship, and let the data decide on the form taken by the adjustment dynamics of one to the other.[1]

---

1. These studies of consumption function have been explored at great length in the methodology literature. See, in particular, Gilbert 1991, and McElroy 1991, who offer different interpretations on the issue of what is really being tested here. For some recent models in the area, see, for example, Quah 1990, Blundell, Browning, and Meghir 1991.

When Predictions Succeed

So what if the predictions succeed? Here the standard pre-scription—not always lived up to in practice—is that any assessment of the degree of support given to the theory must turn crucially on two questions:

• Are there any competing and interesting alternatives, and if so, has the theory been tested against these?

• What is the power of the statistical test used in discrim-inating between these rival theories?

Beyond these rules of the game, there are a number of broader issues that deserve attention in this area:

1. Sometimes, the most interesting alternative to a highly structured classical model is a model of a more primitive kind. It may be that the apparently successful prediction emanating from a highly structured model would follow from a less highly structured model that embodied some basic features.

Many years ago, Gary Becker gave one of the simplest and best-known examples of this problem when he noted that the observation that demand curves are downward slop-ing tells us nothing about conventional demand theory: a primitive behavioral model will, given the budget con-straints faced by consumers, generate downward-sloping demand schedules.

A more striking example, where a familiar relation that is generally thought of as arising from a classical model of individual maximizing is instead traced to a different source, is provided by Hildenbrand's work on the law of demand.[4] Hildenbrand shows that the law of demand can emerge at the aggregate level in a model where individual agents are not assumed to obey the law, simply as a result of aggregation across a large number of heterogeneous agents (Hildenbrand 1994).

2. In listing the competing models that are plausible a priori, it may be that we find that the list is long and unwieldly. We may also find that the interesting questions turn, not on the choice of one (fully specified) model against another, but, rather, on whether the model(s) that describe the data do or do not involve some economically relevant feature. When this is so, it may be more helpful to look directly at the predictions common to the class of models that share this feature. This brings us away from the goal of listing a set of fully specified competing models, in favor of adopting the class-of-models approach of chapter 3.

The Strong Interpretation

In the light of the difficulties we so often encounter in selecting one fully specified model over another, it is

---

4. The law of demand states that for any two price vectors, $\mathbf{p} = (p_1, p_2, \ldots, p_n)$ and $\mathbf{p}' = (p_1', p_2', \ldots, p_n')$ and the associated demands $F(\mathbf{p}) = (q_1, q_2, \ldots, q_n)$ and $F(\mathbf{p}') = (q_1', q_2', \ldots, q_n')$,

$$(\mathbf{p} - \mathbf{p}') \cdot (F(\mathbf{p}) - F(\mathbf{p}')) < 0.$$

In other words, the vector of price changes and the vector of demand changes point in opposite directions.

important to draw a distinction between the two interpretations of the standard paradigm set out in chapter 1.
On the weak interpretation, the paradigm provides us
with a diagnostic technique that helps us to uncover any
systematic economic mechanisms that underlie the patterns that we see in the data. This leaves open the question
of whether the market lends itself to a representation in
terms of a "complete" model in which there is a sharp
separation between a small number of measurable factors
that exert a large and systematic effect on outcomes and
those remaining noise factors, whose influence is both
small and random. The strong interpretation of the paradigm posits that there is some true model of this latter
kind; if this is so, then all researchers—and all the
agents in the market or economy—should be able to identify and agree upon what this model is. This viewpoint
carries important—and controversial—implications (box
4.2).

The Emergence of Pessimism

Testing theories under the standard paradigm is, then, a
tricky business. Among the first generation of economists
who espoused the standard paradigm in the 1950s and
1960s, there was widespread optimism. Much has been
written on the optimistic focus on searching for testable
theories in this period, and on the gradual emergence of
an appreciation of how the problems of model selection
rendered the business of discriminating between rival

theories extremely difficult. (See, for example, the essays in the volume edited by de Marchi 1988.)

The rather mixed track record of research within the standard paradigm over the past generation has led to the emergence of two views, both pessimistic about the possibility of achieving what was taken for granted as the proper goal of economic research in the 1960s: the development of a set of theoretical models, which would rest on a small number of well-motivated assumptions, and which would place clear and testable restrictions on the space of observable outcomes. While this goal is still widely regarded as the right one, it is sometimes seen as asking too much.

The first of the views I want to remark upon is popular among some—but by no means all—theorists. It goes like this: econometric tests of rival theories are notoriously problematic, and often fail to resolve the issue. We therefore need to place a heavy reliance on our judgment as to what factors matter in a situation, as well as on a priori considerations that lead us to model a situation in one way rather than another. This "aesthetic" view—which is, in fact, a reversion to the position set out by Robbins in 1932—is, up to a point, not unreasonable. The problems arise when the argument is pushed a stage further so that the theorist's preferred model is used as a basis for policy recommendations. Rival theorists will always differ in their aesthetic judgments as to what factors are of primary importance in any market, and there seems no way of

Box 4.2
The Strong Interpretation

The strong interpretation of the standard paradigm posits that the market, or the economy, is correctly represented by some true model, whose structure can be uncovered via a model-selection exercise. Under this interpretation, it seems almost compelling to extend our usual notion of rational and well-informed agents to that of agents who are privy to the structure of this true model (they form "rational expectations"). I argue here that this stronger interpretation of the paradigm is warranted only in special circumstances. These circumstances include, for instance, the auctions and options examples of chapter 2. Other circumstances of this kind will occur from time to time, in markets whose characteristics show an unusual degree of stability over time, and in which an unchanging or slowly changing population of agents have acquired reliable experience of the workings of the market in the past.

Matters become more controversial when we move to the more complicated setting of the macro-economy. Here no consensus exists among researchers as to what the true model is. It therefore seems implausible to assume that all the agents in the economy are privy to such a model, and make their decisions accordingly.

Yet, as long as we retain the strong version of the standard paradigm, it is very difficult to escape the logical force of the argument that brings us to a standard rational expectations (R.E.) model. In such a setting, the imposition of expectations-formation mechanisms that contradict the R.E. model raises serious difficulties: could a smart agent not do better by using an R.E. rule? If the agents are not using such a rule, then could the policy maker not exploit

Box 4.2 (continued)

this behavior? Won't the results of such a non–R.E. model themselves be open to the objection that agents will in reality see through such policies? And so on …

But what if there is no true model, in the sense that we cannot pin down the workings of the macroeconomy in the form of some complete model of the classical kind? What if the evidence provided by observables allows us to reject some candidate models, but leaves us with a set of models, none of which can be rejected on the basis of evidence available to the agents in the economy, or to the researcher?

In that case, the internal logic of the situation no longer brings us towards the standard rational expectations setting. Instead, we may think of the agents as taking any one of a range of decisions, each of which is reasonable in the sense that it is optimal relative to some tenable belief about the underlying model.[1]

This looser framework, which is a natural extension of that explored in chapter 3,[2] might be an interesting vehicle to explore, though it lies beyond my present scope. My aim in raising the issue here is to clarify what it is we take on board when we adopt the strong version of the standard paradigm.

1. It is important to emphasize that there is no true model available to some observing researcher relative to which he can evaluate these decisions, and toward which agents' beliefs might converge over time.
2. This setting goes one step beyond the setting explored in chapter 3. There, the problem of observability related only to the researcher; for any particular market, we supposed that there was some true model, and the agents knew that model. Here, we are extending the problem of observability to the agents themselves.

resolving such differences other than by testing the different predictions of rival theories.[5] The later history of policy in relation to San Diego taxicabs offers a nice illustration of how far wrong we can go by appealing to the wrong model. In the absence of some way of testing the claims of rival models, we are left only with some a priori judgments as to what factors matter. In the final analysis, the aesthetic view amounts to an argument from authority.

The second view on which I would like to remark is also a pessimistic one. It goes like this: in many situations of interest, there is a reasonable theory that meets with all those conditions that we might require on a priori grounds, yet it places no nontrivial restrictions on outcomes. In such situations, the only interesting content of the theory lies in the parameter values that we attach to it by means of a standard model-selection exercise. Now, this is quite reasonable, and it is indeed true that there are many situations in which the standard theory fails to impose any interesting restrictions on outcomes. Every student of economics will recall the best-known example: does a rise in the wage rate lead to a rise, or a fall, in labor sup-

---

5. This point should not be pushed too far. We cannot, and should not, need to test a proposed model in each market prior to coming to any policy conclusion about that market. Economics is, after all, about the search for generalizations. The point is that the only models that we should appeal to in making claims as to the likely effects of a policy intervention in some market are those that have been shown empirically to work well for markets with analogous features.

ply? The answer, in theory, is ambiguous; we must let the data decide.[6]

The question is, how typical is this situation? The pessimistic view is that, over the broad run of problems we address, theory is capable only of providing a framework, or a catalog of models which econometricians can use in carrying out parameter estimation. Providing such a framework is a perfectly valid and useful task for theory; yet if this were all that could be delivered, then economic theory would be a poor kind of thing. One of the themes that runs through these chapters is that we can hope for more. In some (and perhaps many) situations, it is possible to find theories that work.

The Paradigm in Perspective

The theme of these chapters is easily summarized: on the one hand, the problems identified by early critics of the standard paradigm are indeed deep and serious, and should not be brushed aside. If we take such worries seriously, we will adopt a relaxed and eclectic view as to research methods, and we will be the better for doing so. Yet, such difficulties notwithstanding, the goal espoused by the

---

6. The reason is that the substitution effect, which leads to a rise in labor supply, may be outweighed by the income effect (richer consumers demand more leisure). Empirically, the consensus is that the net effect is zero for (prime-age) males, and positive for females (viz., higher wages do raise labor supply).

founders of the standard paradigm remains the right, true goal of economic research. For what the birth of the standard paradigm brought into economics was a new insistence on the importance of formulating rival views in the guise of sharply defined theories that could be evaluated by reference to clear empirical tests. It is this, rather than any rigid recipe for research, that remains its enduring legacy.

Notes

Chapter 1

1.1 Keynes versus Tinbergen

In 1939, a short book by J. Tinbergen appeared under the imprint of the League of Nations. Entitled *A Method and Its Application to Investment Activity*, it was billed as the first contribution to a series on the statistical testing of business-cycle theories. The book introduced a style of analysis that would dominate applied macroeconomics for the next generation. It was reviewed in the *Economic Journal* by Keynes, whose tone, though respectful of the author, was deeply skeptical.

Keynes began with an interpretation of what the econometric method might hope to achieve:

Professor Tinbergen agrees that the main purpose of his method is to discover, in cases where the economist has correctly analysed beforehand the qualitative character of the causal relations, with what strength each of them operates.

He goes on to develop his central claim:

Am I right in thinking that the method of multiple correlation analysis essentially depends on the economist having furnished, not merely a list of the significant causes, which is correct so far as it goes, but a *complete* list? For example, suppose three factors are taken into account, it is not enough that these should be in fact verae causae; there must be no other significant factor. If there is a further factor, not taken account of, then the method is not able to discover the relative quantitative important of the first three. If so, this means that the method is only applicable where the economist is able to provide beforehand a correct and indubitably complete analysis of the significant factors. The method is one neither of discovery nor of criticism. It is a means of giving quantitative precision to what, in qualitative terms, we know already as the result of a complete theoretical analysis— provided always that it is a case where the other considerations to be given below are satisfied.

... The next condition is that all the significant factors are measurable,... (and presumably it should be added, that we have adequate statistical knowledge of their measure. Professor Tinbergen states this condition with emphasis, but he does so in terms which do not satisfy me without further explanation. He writes (p. 11)—

The inquiry is, by its nature, restricted to the examination of measurable phenomena. Non-measurable phenomena may, of course, at times exercise an important influence on the course of events; and the results of the present analysis must be supplemented by such information about the extent of that influence as can be obtained from other sources.

He suggests here that the method can be usefully applied if *some* of the factors are measurable, the results obtained from examining these factors being "supplemented" by other information.

But how can this be done? He does not tell us. His method of calculating the relative importance of these measurable factors essentially depends on the assumption that between them they are comprehensive. He gives them such regression coefficients that they completely explain the phenomenon under examination. How can they be "supplemented" by other information?

... If it is necessary that *all* the significant factors should be measurable, this is very important. For it withdraws from the operation of the method all those economic problems where political, social and psychological factors, including such things as government policy, the progress of invention and the state of expectation, may be significant. In particular, it is inapplicable to the problem of the Business Cycle.

In the interchange that followed (Tinbergen 1939), Tinbergen clarified his views on these issues, and in so doing he provided a succinct statement of the robust, "commonsensical" view that was to become the norm among econometricians for the next generation. His statement is worth quoting in full:

To begin with, Mr. Keynes formulates a number of *conditions* which, in his mind, must be fulfilled in order that the method of multiple correlation analysis may be applied. With the formulation he gives on p. 560—viz., that "the most he may be able to show is that, if they (i.e., certain given factors) are *verae causae*, either the factors are not independent or the correlations involved are not linear, or there are other relevant respects in which the economic environment is not homogeneous over a period of time—I find myself only partly in agreement. *I think something more can be shown*, viz. that *in so far as one agrees*

(a) that the explanatory variables chosen explicitly are the relevant ones;

(b) that the non-relevant explanatory variables may be treated as random residuals, not systematically correlated with the other explanatory variables; and

(c) that the mathematical form of the relation is given,

certain details on the probability distributions of their "influences" can be given.... These details are the central (most probable) values and the standard deviations of the regression coefficients, measuring the "influences." In plain terms: these influences can be measured, allowing for certain margins of uncertainty ...

Mr. Keynes goes on to ask: "Am I right in thinking that *the method ... essentially depends on the economist having furnished ... a complete list?*" I think this is right—indeed, it is my condition (a) above—but, as has been stated in §2 of my first volume, it does not matter, if non-relevant factors have been forgotten, and therefore the restriction seems to me far less serious than Mr. Keynes assumes.

What factors are relevant and what are not will not always be clear beforehand. It must then be tried out (cf. §4 below).

As to condition (b), this may be tested afterwards ...

In other words, Tinbergen argues the now-conventional view, that we should propose some model a priori, but be guided by the data in redesigning the model as appropriate—keeping an open mind to the possibility that there may be relevant influences whose role we have not anticipated, and whose possible influence is best gauged by incorporating them in the model and measuring their putative influence.

Tinbergen's reply is eminently sensible and fair; the question, then as now, is whether this kind of investigation will lead us to a correct specification, or whether the role played by unobservables will lead us astray. Throughout the 1950s and 1960s, it appeared that Tinbergen's robust view of these matters had been well justified. In the early 1970s, however, the first oil crisis constituted a serious shock to macroeconomic activity. The large macro-models whose behavior during the 1960s had seemed reasonably stable now mispredicted badly. The general diagnosis ran in terms of the claim that many of these models embodied reduced form relationships rather than structural equations (which by definition were stable vis-à-vis such external shocks). Thus the precise fears that were anticipated by Haavelmo had proved all too real, and Keynes's initial skepticism was now less easy to dismiss.

Chapter 3

3.1 Carnot's Rival

Of the many theorists who devoted attention to the determinants of efficiency in steam engines, the Count de Pambours was particularly well regarded by his contemporaries. His style of theorizing met with the approval of engineers, who favored his elaboration of a complex and complete description of relevant factors. This led to a rather daunting system of equations and to an appeal to experimentally determined parameter values, which, in conjunction with the equations of the system, permitted a "point estimate" of the efficiency of operation of a particular engine. That estimate, given in the 1838 English translation of his book, nicely conveys the difference in his line of attack vis-à-vis that of Carnot (Guyonneau de Pambours, 1838).

3.2 Carnot's Theory of Heat

Carnot's theory was, paradoxically, based on a widely held but incorrect theory of the nature of heat: the "law of conservation of caloric." Feynman, Leighton, and Sands 1963, volume 1, chapter 44, remark that Carnot's argument is subtle, and correct, while the restatement by Clausius in 1850—which states the (false) law of conservation of caloric explicitly—is in error. However, the growing acceptance in the years immediately following publication of Carnot's book, that caloric was not conserved, appears to have caused Carnot some concern as to the standing of his results. While most of his papers were burned following his early death from cholera out of fear of infection, some notes survive—and these notes are heavily preoccupied with the consequences of the failure of the law of conservation of caloric (Maury 1986).

References

Aitcheson, J., and J. A. C. Brown. (1966). *The Lognormal Distribution.* Cambridge: Cambridge University Press.

Atkins, P. W. (1984). *The Second Law: Energy, Chaos, and Form.* New York: Scientific American Books.

Backhouse, Roger E. (1995). *Interpreting Macroeconomics: Explorations in the History of Macroeconomic Thought.* London: Routledge.

Bain, J. (1956). *Barriers to New Competition.* Cambridge, MA: Harvard University Press.

Barten, A. P. and L. J. Bettendorf. (1989). "Price Formation of Fish: An Application of an Inverse Demand System." *European Economic Review*, vol. 33, pp. 1509–1525.

Black, F., and M. Scholes. (1973). "The Pricing of Options and Corporate Liabilities." *Journal of Political Economy*, vol. 81, pp. 637–654.

Blundell, Richard W., Martin J. Browning, and Costas Meghir. (1991). "Consumer Demand and the Lifetime Allocation of Household Expenditure." University College London, unpublished.

Cardwell, D. S. L. (1989). *From Watt to Clausius: The Rise of Thermodynamics in the Early Industrial Age.* Ames: Iowa University Press.

Carnot, S. (1824). *Réflexions sur la puissance motrice du feu.* Paris. (An English translation is available as *Reflexions on the Motive Power of Fire,* E. Mendoza (ed.), New York, 1960.)

Coase, R. H. (1994). *Essays on Economics and Economists.* Chicago: University of Chicago Press.

Cohen, W. M., and Levin, R. C. (1989). "Innovation and Market Structure." In *Handbook of Industrial Organisation,* vol. 2, edited by R. Schmalensee and R. Willig. Amsterdam: North Holland.

Cohen, W. M., Levin, R. C., and Mowery, D. C. (1987). "Firm Size and R&D Intensity: A Re-examination." *Journal of Industrial Economics,* vol. 35, pp. 543–563.

Cox, John C., Stephen A. Ross, and Mark Rubinstein. (1979). "Option Pricing: A Simplified Approach." *Journal of Financial Economics,* vol. 7, pp. 229–263.

Davidson, James, E. H., David F. Hendry, Frank Sraba, and Stephen Yeo. (1978). "Econometric Modelling of the Aggregate Time-Series Relationship between Consumers' Expenditure and Income in the United Kingdom." *Economic Journal,* vol. 88, pp. 661–692.

De Marchi, N. (1988). *The Popperian Legacy in Economics, papers presented at a symposium in Amsterdam, December 1985.* Cambridge: Cambridge University Press.

Deaton, Angus. (1992). *Understanding Consumption.* Oxford: Clarendon Press.

Dow, Christopher. (1998). *Major Recessions.* Oxford: Oxford University Press.

Duesenberry, James S. (1949). *Income, Saving and the Theory of Consumer Behaviour*. Cambridge, MA: Harvard University Press.

Englebrecht-Wiggans, R., P. Milgrom, and R. Weber. (1982). "Competitive Bidding and Proprietary Information." *Journal of Mathematical Economics*, vol. 11, pp. 161–169.

Feynman, Richard P., Robert B. Leighton, and Matthew Sands. (1963). *The Feynman Lectures on Physics*, vol. 1. Reading, MA: Addison Wesley.

Finnerty, J. (1978). "The Chicago Board Options Exchange and Market Efficiency." *Journal of Financial and Quantitative Analysis*, March 1978, pp. 29–38.

Friedman, Milton. (1957). *A Theory of the Consumption Function*. Princeton: Princeton University Press.

Gemill, Gordon. (1993). *Option Pricing: An International Perspective*. New York: McGraw-Hill.

Gilbert, Christopher. (1991). "Do Economists Test Theories? Demand Analysis and Consumption Analysis as Tests of Theories of Economic Methodology." In N. DeMarchi and M. Blaug (eds.), *Appraising Economic Theories*. London: Edward Elgar.

Gujarati, Damodar. (1972a). "The Behaviour of Unemployment and Unfilled Vacancies: Great Britain, 1958–1971." *Economic Journal*, vol. 82, pp. 195–204.

Gujarati, Damodar. (1972b). "A Reply to Mr. Taylor." *Economic Journal*, vol. 82, pp. 1365–1368.

Guyonneau de Pambour, Francois Marie. (1838). *A New Theory of the Steam Engine, and the mode of calculation by means of the effective power 8c. of every kind of steam engine, stationary or locomotive*. London: John Weale.

Haavelmo, T. (1944). "The Probability Approach in Econometrics." *Econometrica*, vol. 12, supplement.

Hall, Robert E. (1978). "Stochastic Implications of the Life Cycle–Permanent Income Hypothesis: Theory and Evidence." *Journal of Political Economy*, vol. 96, pp. 971–987.

Hendricks, K., and R. Porter. (1988). "An Empirical Study of an Auction with Asymmetric Information." *American Economic Review*, vol. 78, pp. 865–883.

Hendry, David. (1993). *Econometrics: Alchemy or Science?* Oxford: Blackwell.

Hendry, David. (1983). "Econometric Modelling: The Consumption Function in Retrospect." *Scottish Journal of Political Economy*, vol. 30, pp. 193–200.

Hull, John C. (1989). *Options, Futures, and Other Derivatives*. Englewood Cliffs, N. J.: Prentice Hall.

Hildenbrand, Werner. (1994). *Market Demand*. Princeton: Princeton University Press.

Hills, Richard. (1989). *Power from Steam: A History of the Stationary Steam Engine*. Cambridge: Cambridge University Press.

Johnstone, J. (1923). *An Introduction to Oceanography with Special Reference to Geography and Geophysics*. London: Hodder & Stoughton Ltd.

Keynes, J. M. (1939). "Review of J. Tinbergen (1939). *Statistical Testing of Business Cycle Theories*, vol. 1, Geneva: League of Nations." *Economic Journal*, vol. 49, pp. 558–568.

Keynes, J. M. (1940). "Professor Tinbergen's Method, Comment." *Economic Journal*, vol. 50, pp. 141–156.

Laffont, J.-J. (1997). "Game Theory and Empirical Economics: The Case of Auction Data." *European Economic Review*, vol. 41, pp. 1–36.

Latané, H., and R. J. Rendleman, Jr. (1976). "Standard Deviations of Stock Price Returns Implied in Option Prices." *Journal of Finance*, vol. 31, pp. 369–382.

Leamer, E. E. (1983). "Let's Take the Con Out of Econometrics." *American Economic Review*, vol. 73, pp. 31–43.

Lupro, Barbara. (1993). "San Diego's Experiences with Taxicab Rates of Fare." Paper presented to the NATR Conference.

Lyons, B., and C. Matraves. (1996). "Industrial Concentration." In S. Davis and B. Lyons (eds.), *Industrial Organisation in the European Union*, chapter 6. Oxford: Oxford University Press.

Lyons, B., Matraves, C., and Moffat, P. (2000). "Industrial Concentration and Market Integration in the European Union." *Economics*, forthcoming

Mandelbrot, Benoit. (1964). "The Variation of Certain Speculative Prices." In Paul H. Cootner (ed.), *The Random Character of Stock Market Prices*. Cambridge, MA: MIT Press.

Mandelbrot, Benoit B. (1997). *Fractals and Scaling in Finance: Discontinuity, Concentration, Risk*. New York: Springer.

Maury, Jean-Pierre. (1986). *Carnot et la machine a vapeur*. Paris: Presses Universitaires de France.

Mayer, T. (1972). *Permanent Income, Wealth, and Consumption*. Berkeley: University of California Press.

McElroy, Marjorie B. (1991). "Comment on Gilbert." In N. DeMarchi and M. Blaug (eds.), *Appraising Economic Theories*. London: Edward Elgar.

Melchior, P. (1983). *The Tides of the Planet Earth*. Oxford: Pergamon Press.

Merton, R. C. (1973). "Theory of Rational Option Pricing." *Bell Journal of Economics and Management Science*, vol. 4, pp. 141–183.

Milgrom, Paul. (1998). "Game Theory and the Spectrum Auctions." *European Economic Review*, vol. 42, pp. 771–778.

Morgan, M. (1986). "Finding a Satisfactory Empirical Model." In *The Popperian Legacy in Economics, papers presented at a symposium in Amsterdam, December 1985*, N. de Marchi (ed.), Cambridge: Cambridge University Press.

Morgan, M. (1987). "Statistics without Probability and Haavelmo's Revolution in Econometrics." In *The Probabilistic Revolution, Volume 2: Ideas in the Sciences*, Lorenz Kruger, Gerd Gigerenzer, and Mary S. Morgan (eds.), London: MIT Press.

Pigou, A. C. (ed.) (1925). *Memorials of Alfred Marshall*. London: Macmillan and Co.

Pugh, D. T. (1989). *Tides, Surges and Mean Sea Level*. New York: John Wiley and Sons.

Quah, Danny. (1990). "Permanent and Transitory Movements in Labour Income: An Explanation for "Excess Smoothness" in Consumption." *Journal of Political Economy*, vol. 98, pp. 449–475.

Rees, A. (1820). *The Cyclopaedia: or Universal Dictionary of Arts, Sciences and Literature*. London: Longman, Hurst, Rees, Orme & Brown.

Robbins, L. (1932). *An Essay on the Nature and Significance of Economic Science*. London: Macmillan.

Robinson, W., and J. Chiang. (1996). "Are Sutton's Predictions Robust? Empirical Insights into Advertising, R&D and Concentration." *Journal of Industrial Economics*, vol. 44, pp. 389–408.

Salop, Steven, and Joseph Stiglitz. (1977). "Bargains and Ripoffs: A Model of Monopolistic Competitive Price Dispersion. *"Review of Economic Studies,"* vol. 44, pp. 493–510.

Shaked, Avner, and John Sutton. (1987). "Product Differentiation and Industrial Structure." *Journal of Industrial Economics*, vol. 36(2).

Sutton, J. (1991). *Sunk Costs and Market Structure.* Cambridge, MA: MIT Press.

Sutton, J. (1993). "Echoes of Edgeworth: The Problem of Indeterminacy." *European Economic Review*, vol. 2/3, pp. 491–499.

Sutton, J. (1998). *Technology and Market Structure.* Cambridge, MA: MIT Press.

Taylor, Jim. (1972). "The Behaviour of Unemployment and Unfilled Vacancies: Great Britain, 1958–1971. An Alternative View." *Economic Journal*, vol. 82, pp. 1352–1365.

Tinbergen, J. (1939). *Statistical Testing of Business Cycle Theories*, vols. 1 and 2. Geneva: League of Nations.

Tinbergen, J. (1940). "A Method of Statistical Business-Cycle Research: A Reply" (with a reply by J. M. Keynes). *Economic Journal*, vol. 50, 141–156.

von Hayek, F. A. (1942). "Scientism and the Study of Society." *Economica*, vol. 9, pp. 267–291.

von Hayek, F. A. (1989). "The Pretence of Knowledge." *American Economic Review (Papers and Proceedings)*, vol. 79, no. 6.

Weverbergh, M. (1979). "Competitive Bidding with Asymmetric Information Reanalysed." *Management Science*, vol. 25, pp. 291–294.

Whaley, R. (1982). "Valuation of American Call Options on Dividend-Paying Stocks." *Journal of Financial Economics*, vol. 10, pp. 29–58.

Wheeler, W. H. (1906). *A Practical Manual of Tides and Waves*. London: Longmans, Green & Co.

Whitaker, John K. (1996). *The Correspondence of Alfred Marshall, Economist, vol. 2. At the Summit 1981–1902*. Cambridge: Cambridge University Press.

Wilson, R. (1967). "Competitive Bidding with Asymmetric Information." *Management Science*, vol. 13, pp. 816–820.

Index